Exercising for Excellence

Exercising for Excellence

Delivering successful business continuity
management exercises

Crisis Solutions

CRISIS SOLUTIONS

BSi
Business
Information

First published in the UK in 2008
by
BSI
389 Chiswick High Road
London W4 4AL

Typeset in Frutiger by Monolith – http://www.monolith.uk.com
Printed in Great Britain by The MFK Group, Stevenage

British Library Cataloguing in Publication Data
A catalogue record for this book is available from the British Library

ISBN 978 0 580 50953 7

Contents

Contents

Foreword

The largest simulation exercise I had ever been involved in was about to start. I was in a glass-fronted room in a tower block overlooking London with close to 100 people; the exercise command centre and the hub of what was about to unfold. A young man in a dark business suit rose to his feet and said, 'We go live in 10 seconds.' A hush descended on the room, which was abruptly broken by the insistent music of a simulated TV news bulletin. All over London, elsewhere in the UK and across the world, more than 80 corporate crisis teams were simultaneously seeing the same internet-streamed news and the exercise was underway.

Our purpose was to test the resilience of a vital part of critical national infrastructure and, as exercise director, ultimate responsibility for running the event rested with me. Given the government departments and the global companies involved it was pretty clear, success was the only acceptable outcome. To add to the pressure, international observers were in attendance so the stakes were high for everyone concerned.

A real first for this event was the way the internet was used to create a multi-channel interactive experience for the participants so that, during the course of the exercise, more than 2,000 players from over 80 companies were able to rehearse their roles in a highly realistic environment. A series of live websites were created to give all the players the same information at exactly the same time, representing news media, financial data and information from the emergency services.

During the three-hour exercise, the websites handled more than 15 gigabytes of data on more than 200 pages. The financial data site contained 480 constantly changing graphs and, on average, there was a page update every two minutes. There were also around 3,500 downloads of individual video files from the news site. By the end of the exercise all the corporate teams had had the opportunity to rehearse their role and were better able to understand how their planned responses influenced or were influenced by others' actions. Participant feedback was highly positive and the post-exercise report identified valuable lessons that were subsequently embedded within the exercise participant community so that resilience was enhanced. Success had been achieved!

When contacted by the British Standards Institution to put this book together, I was inevitably drawn to reflect on that exercise and the many others in which I have been involved and how best to share that experience. Although the example

Foreword

cited above was huge in every sense, the principles for success apply to the range of different exercises that you might consider running for your organization. This is because what holds true for a global simulation also holds true for an in-house desktop exercise. So what are the key principles of delivering an effective exercise? A strong planning process, meticulous attention to detail and actionable reporting are the foundations for success – and I hope that the content of this book will help you to achieve your goals.

Scarcely a week goes by when I am not involved in some form of exercise. It may be the way I earn my living, but I do it because I believe in it. In our increasingly uncertain times your organization needs to be ready to respond to disruptive challenges and demonstrate preparedness to employees, clients, customers, regulators and shareholders.

This book represents a huge amount of knowledge garnered by myself and my colleagues at Crisis Solutions and I am indebted to them for their support. I would like to acknowledge the contributions of Jim Preen, Alistair Cartwright, Peter Brown, Russell Newmarch and Emma Perry. We know that the approaches, processes and procedures contained here work: we use them every day. Now we want them to work for you.

Dennis Flynn
CEO, Crisis Solutions

Introduction

This book should be read in conjunction with *BS 25999-1:2006, Business continuity management: Code of practice*, which sets out the processes, principles and terminology of business continuity management. The book is intended for use by anyone with responsibility for the planning and delivery of exercises. Where no plan exists, an exercise can be the ideal approach to defining the requirement.

Exercises that are properly designed and carried out will develop your people's capabilities, and test your technical, logistical, administrative and procedural systems. Do the members of your nominated crisis management team (CMT) understand their roles and responsibilities? Do they understand the tools available to support effective delivery of a timely response? Does your call-cascade system work? Do you even have a call-cascade? If not, how are you going to find the staff you need to get you through a crisis? Think about it this way: would your senior executives prefer to find the answers to these questions during a major incident or in the controlled environment of an exercise?

Above all, an exercise should enable everyone to understand an organization's current incident management capability. It can demonstrate areas of strengths but can also highlight elements of your planning that are incomplete or need changing. As such, an exercise can be a powerful argument for additional top-down engagement and resources. If your plan is in good shape an exercise will generate high levels of confidence throughout your organization that you are well placed to withstand the impact of disruptions.

About this book

Ideally, exercises should not take place in isolation, but should be part of an ongoing programme. It would be a great mistake to run a plan test, consider your business continuity plan (BCP) validated and the job done. Organizations change, sometimes at a furious rate, and if that is the case then plans will need to evolve and develop at the same pace. Exercises should be part of your planned ongoing maintenance programme as opposed to culminating events.

Chapter 1 looks at the importance of developing an exercise programme and at the challenges of getting senior management on board to endorse and pay for it. British Standard *25999* places exercises into the following categories: simple, medium and complex. Taking this as its starting point, Chapter 2 looks at the importance of choosing the right type of exercise, from a simple desktop to a full-blown crisis simulation that may involve your incident management teams, plus members of the emergency services and the media.

Chapter 3 deals with planning an exercise from scenario development right up to the point of delivery. It analyses the roles of participants and how an exercise should be constructed using a master events list (MEL) to allow for a fast-paced, challenging and fun event. In Chapter 4 we look at the actual delivery of an exercise: how all the players should be briefed, and what event protocols should be in place. It also includes invaluable checklists to help make sure nothing is forgotten.

Finally, Chapter 5 deals with the all-important task of writing the exercise report. There is little point in running an exercise if the data it produces is not collated, digested and understood. Only then can individuals and teams look at their performance in a dispassionate way and plan the way ahead.

Plan tests, exercises and simulations should always be challenging. But planning, developing and running them can sometimes seem even more daunting. With the help of this book some of the sting should be taken out of the planning and delivery. This book provides a straightforward guide that is practical, is not overly concerned with theory, and contains many real-life case studies from people whose livelihood it is to run such exercises.

You will be taken on a journey from the inception of an exercise programme, right through to running an event and beyond. Getting senior management interested in business continuity is often a challenge. This book will help you to deliver a well-run exercise that can raise consciousness from the boardroom to the shop floor and help make the work of those in business continuity valued and understood.

1. Establishing a successful exercise programme

'We may need to solve problems not by removing the cause but by designing the way forward even if the cause remains in place.' Edward de Bono

Introduction

An old saying in business continuity is that having an incident plan can sometimes be worse than having no plan at all – that is, if it has not been effectively tested.

This chapter will help you establish a successful programme to exercise the current business continuity management (BCM) arrangements within your organization. Developing a successful exercise programme will also help you comply with new British Standard *BS 25999*.

> Morgan Stanley's response to the 11 September 2001 attacks on the Twin Towers in New York, where the company had offices, gives us an insight into what a successful exercise programme can achieve. For them, resilience was not just about computer systems recovery; it was all about people and embraced the entire organization.
>
> Continuous exercise and training following the 1993 World Trade Center bombing meant the company had plans and procedures in place that were of enormous value during the terror strike of 9/11.
>
> Most of the company's 3,700 employees survived the evacuation of the south tower. The company then proceeded to re-establish contact with its dispersed employees using house calls, public broadcasts and one of its own call centres in Arizona. Within three days nearly all staff based in the south tower had been located.
>
> While accounting for their personnel was paramount, they also set about recovering business operations at alternative facilities. Three days after the terror attack, testing activities were in progress and the recovery, both physical and emotional, was underway.

The BCM lifecycle

A BCM programme covers all phases of the BCM lifecycle (see Figure 1.1) and must be supported by senior management and appropriately resourced.

BCM arrangements need to be implemented so you can:

- Identify the impact of potential losses
- Maintain viable recovery strategies and plans
- Ensure continuity of products and services through exercise, maintenance and review.

The BCM lifecycle found in *BS 25999* comprises six elements, which can be implemented by organizations of all sizes, in all sectors.

When establishing a successful exercise programme, every part of this cycle must be examined in depth.

The stages of the BCM lifecycle can run in sequence or in parallel depending on your needs. Using the lifecycle should help you identify the purpose and objectives of your exercise programme.

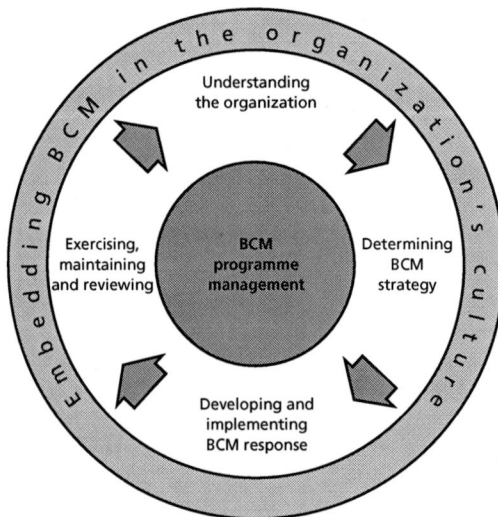

Figure 1.1 – The business continuity lifecycle

BCM programme management

Programme management enables a business continuity capability to be both established (if necessary) and maintained in a manner appropriate to the size and complexity of your organization. The overall exercise programme should parallel the maturity and complexity of your established BCM programme and be tailored to it. This will also aid you in choosing the right type of exercise(s) for your needs.

Understanding your organization

A thorough understanding of your core business activities will help inform your choices when it comes to selecting your business continuity strategies.

Risk assessment will have its role to play here, but continuous research into 'what should happen' – in others words what is standard practice in your organization – and 'what actually does happen' can produce startling results. The two may be worlds apart, with the product of your research enabling you to choose the ingredients for an exercise programme. One that is designed to expose vulnerabilities not previously acknowledged or understood.

Determining business continuity strategy

A range of business continuity strategies will need to be evaluated to protect your company. Those chosen should allow you to continue to deliver key products and services at an acceptable level of operation or to resume delivery of these services within a satisfactory timeframe.

The choices made will take account of the resilience and countermeasures already present within your organization.

Developing a BCM response

Developing and implementing a business continuity response will result in the creation of what can be a variety of different incident plans. Typically they will include business continuity and recovery plans that detail steps to be taken before, during and after an incident to maintain or restore operations.

An exercise programme should be established to test activation and escalation of your plans and procedures. It should also help audit management decisions and check the current state of both your internal and external communications.

Plans must be constantly updated, tested and disseminated throughout your business.

BCM exercising, maintaining and reviewing

A structured exercise programme with defined objectives should allow you to demonstrate the extent to which your strategic plans are complete, current and accurate. It should also enable you to identify opportunities for improvement.

Action plans that result from exercises will help maintain, review and audit your business continuity arrangements.

Embedding BCM in your organization's culture

If BCM is part of your organization's core values, then all stakeholders should have confidence in your ability to cope with disruptions.

Aligning your exercise programme with your organizational culture is vital when seeking 'buy in' from participants during the development and delivery of an exercise. If they cannot see the relevance of what you are asking them to do, they will quickly lose interest.

Exercises can expose vulnerabilities in a weak organizational structure. They can start processes needed to strengthen both internal and external communication and can help improve management decision making during an incident.

A large, well-known German company (for the purposes of this book we will call them Lux Engineering) provides us with an interesting example of an organization that developed an exercise programme as a result of an incident. They were forced to go back and re-examine all aspects of their business continuity arrangements, but, as we will see this had positive results.

The company outsources most of its production to external manufacturers and one of these suppliers experienced an incident that resulted in 6 months of delivery delays. Lux suffered business interruption costs of over $200 million.

The task Lux set itself was to align its incident plans with those of its suppliers and then validate them using a series of exercises. Only by doing this could it test the resilience of the supply chain network.

The exercises indicated that an innovative approach was needed and resulted in what is known as a 'Risk Management Evaluation Tool'. In short, the tool Lux developed was able to monitor suppliers, ensuring they had contingency plans in place that would, as far as possible, guarantee supply.

The lessons to be drawn from this case study are that risk assessment is an ongoing task and that a carefully designed exercise programme can illuminate vulnerabilities before they turn into an incident. Lux found out the hard way, but as a result of the incident came up with an inventive solution to an ongoing problem.

What can exercising achieve?

The exercising element of the business continuity lifecycle (BCL) is where your business continuity plan is tested and audited and subject to change management.

As stated in *BS 25999*, the exercise programme should:

- Exercise the technical, logistical, administrative, procedural and other operational systems of the BCP
- Exercise the BCM arrangements and infrastructure (including roles, responsibilities, and any incident management locations and work areas, etc.)
- Validate the technology and telecommunications recovery, including the availability and relocation of staff.

In addition it may have the added benefits of:

- Practising the organization's ability to recover from an incident
- Validating the effectiveness and timeliness of restoration of your critical activities
- Verifying that all critical activities are covered by your current plans
- Highlighting assumptions in your plans that need to be questioned
- Instilling confidence amongst exercise participants
- Raising awareness of business continuity throughout your organization
- Demonstrating competence of your primary response teams and their alternatives.

How to develop the exercise programme

To achieve the tasks alluded to in the previous section, you will need an exercise programme management team (EPMT), either temporary or permanent, to oversee the development of the exercise programme.

The roles and responsibilities within this team will need to be clearly defined, as will the resources they require.

The exercise programme management team

The EPMT should have:

- The correct level of authority
- Common focus to ensure the exercise programme succeeds
- Ample BCM experience
- Sufficient time to develop the exercise programme.

They must ensure that:

- Their governance is clearly defined and their roles and responsibilities are documented
- All other stakeholders understand their roles and responsibilities within the exercise programme
- The exercise programme is agreed by all parties involved before exercises get underway.

The team may look something like this:

- Senior management – a senior member of your organization who has a stake in BCM
- Depending on the size of your organization and your circumstances – one or two members of your business continuity team who will use the action plans that result from the exercise programme to improve your business continuity plans
- If no such department exists then recruit members of staff with risk management or business continuity credentials
- If no such persons exist you may wish to consider outside contractors.

It is the job of the senior management member of the team to act as overall sponsor of the programme and to see it is allocated the priority and resources it needs. The business continuity professionals will provide the expertise and will produce the exercise programme proposal.

Once an exercise programme has been defined, members of this team may well become part of the exercise planning group (EPG) as outlined in Chapter 3.

The exercise programme document

An exercise programme document must:

- State the aims and objectives of the exercise programme
- Outline the exercises that will be needed to accomplish these objectives
- Be continually referred to once exercises get underway to check objectives are being met
- Acknowledge that if any significant part of the programme is to be changed then exercise specifications will be altered to reflect this.

A series of exercise specification documents will be contained in an exercise programme document and should be like this:

Exercise Specification Document

Opening page:

- Executive Summary – a one-page outline of the exercise purpose, objectives, exercise programme milestones and budget requirements.

First section:

- Why this exercise is necessary and how it fits within the overall exercise programme
- What the exercise hopes to achieve – its aims and objectives.

Second section:

- Type of exercise – simple, medium or complex. This is dealt with extensively in Chapter 2 but here you should outline the type of exercise chosen and briefly justify your choice.
- The Exercise – a brief outline of what the exercise will contain including possible scenarios. These will be developed further, once the exercise planning is underway.

Third section:

- The exercise timeline – for example: when the scenario will be finalized, when the MEL should be complete. When the exercise report is due and when other exercise documentation can be expected. The milestone timings for each stage of the exercise should be tabulated for quick and easy reference.

Final section:

- Agreement page – agreement and sign off of the proposal by project sponsor.

Appendices:

- Stakeholders – a list of the exercise programme management team members and an outline of their roles and responsibilities
- Budget requirements – a breakdown of estimated costs
- Any other relevant documentation.

The Exercise Specification Document is just a suggested list of sections that can be changed to reflect your circumstances (see Chapter 3 for case study for a completed exercise specification document).

Benefits of a successful exercise programme

An exercise programme should:

- Identify the impacts of an operational disruption or incident
- Exercise the effects and impacts of the disruption
- Demonstrate the effectiveness of your incident plans to deal with the disruption
- Change and update a plan as outlined in a report's action plan
- Help develop an incident plan if no plan exists
- Maintain a tested ability to manage uninsurable risks
- Promote a company-wide approach to business continuity.

The benefits should help promote management and participant 'buy in'.

Senior management 'buy in'

The job of a business continuity professional is made infinitely easier if BCM is actively supported and promoted by senior management.

One of the tasks of the exercise programme management team will be to justify the programme's benefits to senior management. They will need to be fully prepared and briefed to defend the time, money and effort itemized in the document.

Education and fear of the unknown should be the twin drivers used when seeking senior management support for an exercise programme.

Without being unduly pessimistic, it is often a case of 'when' an incident will strike and not 'if' given the current climate of changing technologies and threats – both physical and virtual.

Business continuity must be instilled as a core value in your organization.

Participant 'buy in'

If senior management are on board then those participating in an exercise are more likely to be compliant. An exercise can seem a rather plastic, unreal or just plain alarming experience.

However, if the scenario has been correctly developed and the logistics are in place, then players should become so wrapped up in events as to forget any misgivings they may have harboured.

In Chapter 4, in the 'Day of the exercise' section, we will look closely at how to engage and inspire the players.

How much is this going to cost?

The most compelling way of justifying the programme budget is to compare it to the cost of the consequences of not having a programme at all.

The results of an incident can be far-reaching and might involve loss of life, loss of assets or income, or the inability to deliver products and services on which your organization's survival might depend.

Establishing a successful exercise programme

One company that inadvertently gave an object lesson in how not to respond to an incident was Perrier. By the late 1980s, bottled water was very popular and Perrier was a leading brand.

The company found traces of the chemical benzene in its water and initially did nothing about it, playing the incident down.

When Perrier, in France, realized it did have a problem its first response was to blame employees for incorrectly using benzene cleaning products.

The company's American arm acted very differently and started recalling bottles. Back in France this was seen as alarmist and unhelpful, with the Americans overreacting.

The Perrier share price went into freefall, so that finally, four days after discovering the traces of benzene, all bottles were withdrawn worldwide.

At the time, Perrier was quoted as saying that 'with this action we have saved the image of Perrier all over the world.' Wishful thinking on their part. Perrier's image had already been tarnished. People buy bottled water because it is perceived as being pure and healthy and somehow tasting better than tap water. These were claims it was now hard for Perrier to make.

The company had already broken one of the major rules in press relations as two arms of the company had been saying and doing completely different things: the Americans pulling the bottles, and the French hoping the incident would go away. Combine that with apparent indifference over public health, and you would have thought that things could get no worse.

Perrier had other ideas. Once the scare was over and their water was benzene-free, Perrier started to market again. Much to customers' surprise, the new bottles were smaller, but cost roughly the same price. We have had an incident, the company seemed to be saying, but the customers are the ones that will pay.

Perrier, in its original form, never recovered. Its share price was in tatters leaving it vulnerable to takeover. Nestlé duly obliged.

Possible problems

There are many things that can go wrong with an exercise programme. Problems may arise with personnel and resources. Indeed those involved may have different ideas as to how things should be organized, which makes it vitally important that all are clear about their responsibility, authority and accountability. If everyone is clear about their role, there should be less confusion about the outcome.

Here are some potential exercise programme mishaps:

- Insufficient attention to the objectives and required output contained in the exercise specification document
- Insufficient research into business processes
- Lack of understanding of roles and responsibilities within the exercise programme team
- Poor estimation of time and cost
- Inadequate planning and coordination of resources
- Lack of control over the progress of the programme
- Lack of quality control, resulting in poor exercise delivery.

What have I learnt from this chapter?

- The business continuity lifecycle (BCL) must be reflected in your exercise programme
- The importance of establishing what your organization wants to get out of an exercise programme
- How to populate an exercise programme management team
- What constitutes an exercise specification document.

---

2. Choosing the right type of exercise

'Never tell people how to do things. Tell them what to do and they will surprise you with their ingenuity'. General George Smith Patton, Jr

Exercising is not training

Having established why exercising is necessary and looked at its part in the BCL, we now examine what options are open to your EPMT or anyone else considering what type of exercise to choose.

Before doing so, the difference between training and exercising must be appreciated, as they are not one and the same. Training provides individuals or teams with the skills they require to perform defined roles. Exercising tests whether plans, procedures, processes and structures are fit for purpose.

An individual can receive training on how to compile an events log – recording events, decisions, actions and tasks. An exercise will test whether the processes for obtaining, recording, displaying and reviewing information on the events log adequately supports decision makers and provides an accurate audit trail for future scrutiny.

Exercises are not, and never should be, a test of individuals.

Types of exercises

All exercises are bespoke and are tailored for specific participants for specific reasons. The benefit of categorizing exercises is that it gives planners an immediate idea of scale, complexity and planning effort required for different types of events. To this end, *BS 25999-1* gives a table of 'Types and methods of exercising BCM strategies' which is reproduced in Table 2.1.

These definitions provide broad guidance to the types of available exercise, but it should be recognized that there can be considerable 'blurring of the edges'. It is possible to conduct a simple exercise at a recovery site, adding a different dimension, but this would not necessarily make it a medium exercise. Regardless of the category, the importance of an exercise is that it achieves its defined objectives.

Table 2.1

Complexity	Exercise	Process	Variants	Good practice frequency
Simple	Desk check	Review/ amendment of content Challenge content of BCP	Update/ validation Audit/ verification	At least annually
Medium	Walk-through of plan	Challenge content of BCP	Include interaction and validate participants' roles	Annually
	Simulation	Use 'artificial' situation to validate that the BCP(s) contains both necessary and sufficient information to enable a successful recovery	Incorporate associated plans	Annually or twice a year
	Exercise critical activities	Invocation in a controlled situation that does not jeopardize business as usual operation	Defined operations from alternate site for a fixed time	Annually or less
Complex	Exercise full BCP, including incident management	Building-/ campus-/ exclusion zone-wide exercise		Annually or less

Simple exercises

A simple exercise is often called a 'desktop' or 'workshop'. It typically involves a small number of people, perhaps 5–20, and concentrates on a specific aspect of a BCP or a specific subject area (for example, Human Resources, Information Technology or Media). However, the beauty of a simple exercise is that it can easily accommodate complete teams from various areas of your business. The numbers may increase (and with it the logistics) but the objectives will remain the same.

Alternatively it could involve a single representative from several teams rather than needing the whole team to attend. It will seldom involve the provision of a virtual world environment or the need for other than everyday resources. Typically, participants will be given a simple scenario and then be invited to discuss specific aspects of a company's BCP.

For example, a fire is discovered out of working hours; what are the current call-out procedures? How is the incident management team activated? Where does it meet? Do the current documented procedures cover all eventualities?

It will probably last no more than three hours and is often split into two or three sessions, each concentrating on a different theme. In this case either two or three different scenarios can be used, or one scenario can be progressively developed to introduce themes that need to be addressed. Real time pressure is not usually an element of simple exercises.

Questions will need to be crafted ahead of time so that facilitators ensure discussions are productive and germane to the objectives of the event.

How long will it take to plan? Just because it is a simple exercise does not mean that the planning and preparation can be less thorough. However, in most cases the planning effort will be in the region of days rather than weeks.

Medium exercises

A medium exercise will invariably be conducted within a virtual world and will usually bring together several departments, teams or disciplines. It will typically concentrate on more than one aspect of the BCP prompting interaction between teams.

The scope of a medium exercise can range from a small number of teams from one organization being co-located in one building to multiple teams operating

---

from dispersed locations. Attempts should be made to create as realistic an environment as possible and the numbers of participants should reflect a realistic situation. Depending on the degree of realism required it may be necessary to produce simulated news broadcasts, together with simulated websites.

A medium exercise will normally last between two and three hours, though they can take place over several days.

They typically involve a scenario cell who feed in pre-scripted injections through-out the exercise to give information and prompt actions. This aspect will be expanded in Chapter 3.

The total planning effort will depend largely on the complexity of the scenario and the number of different aspects of the BCP or organization being addressed. For small scale exercises a total of 10 working days spread over two to three months might be sufficient. However, with large scale exercises, 20 to 30 working days might be required over a six month period.

Complex exercises

A complex exercise is perhaps the hardest to define as it aims to have as few boundaries as possible. It will probably incorporate all the aspects of a medium exercise and many more. Elements of the exercise will inevitably have to remain within a virtual world, but every attempt should be made to achieve realism. This might include a no-notice activation, actual evacuation and actual invocation of a disaster recovery (DR) site.

While a start and cut-off time will have to be agreed, the actual duration of the exercise might be unknown if events are allowed to run their course in real time. If it takes two hours to get to the DR site instead of the expected 45 minutes, the exercise must be flexible enough to cater for this. If a key player is unavailable a deputy must be prepared to step in.

The planning effort required for a complex exercise could conceivably be less than that for a medium exercise if the approach adopted is one of 'This event has happened – stand back and see what transpires'.

However, in most cases the planning effort will be at the upper end of that for a medium exercise, that is, at least 20 to 30 working days over a period of up to six months.

Factors to consider

The choice of type of exercise will depend on a number of interrelating factors. Ideally, the EPMT will have considered all of these factors and produced a comprehensive exercise plan which addresses all aspects of the BCP and its implementation. However, if you are not fortunate enough to have such a team, or you have been tasked with organizing an ad hoc exercise, consideration of the following factors will assist you in choosing the right type of exercise for your organization.

Size of organization

When it comes to exercising BCM strategies, is there a difference between a multi-million pound global bank and a family-run bakery? The answer is no! A small company can and should conduct complex exercises if they are to test their plans to the full.

Conversely, complex organizations will need to conduct simple exercises to test discrete aspects of their plans. In this respect, size definitely doesn't matter.

Aims and objectives

The overriding consideration must be the exercise aims and objectives. Why are you doing this exercise and what do you expect to get out of it? Until you have defined, unequivocally, the aims and objectives of the exercise there is no point in going any further in the planning process. They are not just a woolly statement at the beginning of the exercise specification; they define for everyone exactly why you are doing the exercise and will drive every action thereafter. It will require careful thought and ideally, endorsement at the highest level.

If the aims and objectives are 'To validate the content of the pre-planned communications templates', it would not be necessary to involve the complete incident management structure nor to address any aspect of the BCP that does not impinge on communications. In this case a simple exercise would probably suffice.

If, however, the aims and objectives are 'To test the incident management team's current capability to manage a major incident that impacts on the delivery of business as usual', the entire incident management structure would need to be involved and all aspects of the BCP could be addressed. In this case, a simple exercise would be unlikely to achieve this, so a medium or even a complex exercise should be considered.

Experience

An essential factor to consider is the experience levels of those participating in an exercise. It is important that the participants enjoy the exercise and that they learn from it – the last thing you want is to destroy their confidence.

Consideration must be given to whether the proposed participants are capable of delivering the exercise objectives. The exercise is not the place to train individuals in their roles. Ideally this will be addressed in the exercise programme so that inexperienced individuals or teams receive training before taking part in a simple exercise, allowing them to put their training into practice in a controlled environment. Only once this has been successfully achieved should they be exposed to a more pressured medium or complex exercise environment.

Highlighting an individual's inexperience may be an exercise outcome but it can be very demoralising for the person concerned.

At the other end of the spectrum, it is important that experienced individuals and teams are challenged sufficiently to ensure that they remain engaged and also learn from the exercise. They can still participate in simple exercises, but the content of the exercise must reflect the participants' experience and capabilities.

If participants feel patronized or are just repeating what has gone before, their concentration and involvement will quickly lapse.

Previous exercises

When planning a future event, the outcomes of previous exercises should always be considered. While there may be a natural progression from simple through medium to complex exercises, there is no point in pushing on if the objectives have not been met.

If the outcome of the simple exercise example, concerning communications templates, were that the templates were woefully inadequate, there would be little point in progressing to a more complex exercise until the original exercise purpose had been achieved. In this case, a second simple exercise should be conducted before attempting anything more ambitious.

The outcome of previous exercises should also be considered when defining the aims and objectives as issues might have been identified which had not been previously addressed. Conversely it is important that your next exercise presents something new as you will not earn any plaudits for unwittingly reinventing the wheel.

Who do you want to involve?

The type of exercise you choose will usually dictate who will be involved as participants. In general, the more complex the exercise, the more people will be involved. The aims and objectives could also dictate who should participate. Proposed players may demand the inclusion, or exclusion, of specific teams or departments.

Don't over-complicate an exercise by involving people who are not required just to make the exercise seem bigger. While the intention might be to conduct a medium exercise, if the objectives can be met by conducting a simple exercise with fewer participants, then do so. If, however, the exercise objectives can only be met by involving a large number of people from all departments, it will be incumbent on the planners to ensure that the exercise engages all participants sufficiently so that they feel that their participation was worthwhile.

Another factor to consider is the availability of the intended participants. With the possible exception of 'no notice' elements of a complex exercise, business as usual activities should not normally be adversely affected by exercises. It is therefore important that the availability of key players and teams is confirmed before detailed planning commences. In this respect it is useful to have high-level management buy in for the exercise programme as this should help resolve any 'availability' issues.

However, you will not be thanked for planning a finance department exercise during the production of end of year accounts or an exercise to explore strategic decision making processes the morning after the executive Christmas party!

In medium and complex exercises external stakeholders may be involved including the emergency services, DR sites, PR organizations etc. Ensuring their availability will be essential as without them it could be necessary to scale down the exercise as some objectives might be unachievable. The same obviously applies if an external specialist is essential for the delivery of a simple exercise.

Time

Time constraints can also affect the choice of exercise. If it is known that only one hour has been allocated for an exercise, it is unlikely that anything more than a simple exercise could be attempted. Similarly, if a complex exercise is envisaged, it must be confirmed that sufficient time is allocated for its delivery.

And it is not just the time allocated for the exercise – available exercise planning time must be considered. All exercises require, and indeed hinge on thorough planning. As a rule of thumb, however, the more complex the exercise, the more planning effort required. If sufficient planning time is not available to achieve the complexity required, that type of exercise should not be attempted.

Conducting too many exercises of the same type too frequently may engender complacency and stifle progress. Infrequent exercising will also hinder progress as lessons will have to be relearned. Table 2.1 from *BS 25999-1* gives a 'Good practice frequency' for exercising; however, any well designed exercise programme, must be flexible and should reflect the culture and needs of your particular organization.

Planners

Exercises don't plan themselves. When choosing the type of exercise it is essential to ensure that there are sufficient people available to conduct the thorough planning it will involve. Everyone has a 'day job', and so being part of an exercise planning team is likely to be above and beyond what they normally do. It is essential that members of a planning team understand exactly what will be required of them and if they cannot guarantee to deliver, they should not take part.

Simple exercises might only involve one or two planners but as the complexity increases, so will the size of the planning team. In more complex exercises which involve external stakeholders, they will be required to be involved in the planning process and may be vital to the success of the exercise. If they cannot commit to the planning requirement it may be necessary to scale back the scope of the exercise. If in-house resources are clearly not sufficient to plan for the scale of exercise desired, consideration should be given to engaging the services of an external specialist provider.

Case study – Testing the communications team

As we've seen in this chapter, there are many different types of exercise from a simple desktop discussion right through to a full-blown simulation exercise incorporating live play.

In this case study we look at the nuts and bolts of running an exercise dedicated to testing one part of an organization's BCP. This time it is the communications team who are in the spotlight.

The background

As part of its ongoing plan testing strategy a European bank wanted to evaluate the incident communication capabilities of both its internal and external communication teams and allow participants to practise roles and responsibilities in an incident press room.

One of the major challenges when planning the simulation was the number of people involved. Fifty members of communication departments from across Europe had to be tested, stretched, educated and kept involved.

The planning

It was decided that two plausible and challenging news scenarios were required together with a series of injections for each scenario to maintain pressure on the participants. A full-blown MEL was not deemed necessary.

In an incident it is important that communications staff think like reporters – how could that be achieved?

The players were divided into three teams, and each team was then subdivided into two groups. In each team one group played the role of the press room, dealing both with internal and external communications. The other group played the role of journalists, members of staff and members of the public phoning into the press room for information. Each group contained approximately eight people.

Communication between the groups took place using mobile phones. Telephone directories were produced and issued just prior to the start of the exercise.

Each scenario lasted about 45 minutes. When this was completed the groups swapped roles and moved on to scenario two.

At the end of each scenario those in the press room had to produce a press release and a short summary of the messages that the company felt appropriate for release to the media.

Those involved in internal communication were tasked with producing a quick initial holding statement for company staff plus a later, more extended version.

To test the incident readiness of the teams, once both scenarios were complete each team had to nominate a spokesperson to face a television interview. A professional journalist and cameraperson were employed to put them through their paces. They were asked questions based on the scenario in play while they were in the press room.

The delivery

These are the two scenarios that were used:

Scenario 1. 'Heartless' bank killed my son

The Euro-Wide Bank stands accused today of being partially responsible for the death of 37-year-old Jeremy Dobbs. His mother, Angela Dobbs, broke down as she described how her son, a Multiple Sclerosis sufferer who lived on benefits, had taken his own life.

Though very ill and entirely dependent on benefits, EWB lent Mr Dobbs £20,000 which he could never pay back. His mother believes the bank's actions directly contributed to his suicide. The five-year loan, swallowing more than half his monthly benefits, came with costly protection insurance. In view of Michael's long illness and his inability to hold down a job, it was not worth the paper it was written on.

EWB said, 'The loan was granted based on the information that was provided by Mr Dobbs' credit scoring and the conduct of his bank account'. It added: 'EWB has strict lending criteria. It is not in our interest or our customers' interest to lend money that cannot be repaid.'

Yet consumer groups are horrified by the fact that Jeremy was granted such a big loan by a high street bank, even though he was living on benefits. 'It's disgraceful,' says Joe Solomon, chief executive of the Independent Banking Advisory Service. 'This is the most irresponsible piece of lending I've ever come across; they should be ashamed of themselves.'

Solomon says the Government must now urgently rein in the excesses of the banks. 'Irresponsible lending is a major issue that the Government must tackle head on,' he says.

While looking at pictures of her son in happier times Angela Dobbs said, 'I could see him getting more and more depressed – the money seemed to bear down on him. He knew he could never pay it back and felt he was a burden on us. This is the bank that last year made £10 billion in profits. They seem happy to take the money – now they've taken a life.'

To keep the scenario moving, the following injections or incidents were handed to those asking the questions during the course of exercise play.

Scenario 1, Injection 1

A woman in a wheelchair, Mary Jacobson, has been pushed into the EWB branch at 200 Tranter Street, Birmingham, where she has spoken to staff.

She says she has read the newspapers concerning Jeremy Dobbs and is claiming to be in a similar circumstance.

She is disabled, unable to work, lives on benefits and she too has been lent a substantial sum by EWB (£9,000) which she now says she has no chance of repaying.

She claims that she previously made an offer to EWB to pay off the loan at £20 a month, but this was rejected. Currently the loan is costing her over £200 a month.

She is clearly distressed and is demanding help from EWB staff. If help is not forthcoming she says she will go to the press with her story.

* * * * * *

Players will simulate staff at the Birmingham branch phoning in for guidance.

A few minutes later this story leaks to the media.

Scenario 1, Injection 2

A producer from the BBC Radio 4 World at One programme calls the EWB press office.

Joe Solomon, chief executive of the Independent Banking Advisory Service, has agreed to appear on the show to discuss the Dobbs' case and wider issues concerning the lending policy of high street banks. He is expected to be critical of EWB.

EWB are invited to field someone to put their case.

* * * * * *

Injection to be handed to a 'journalist' who will assume the role of the World at One producer – a forthright individual who won't let EWB off the hook and points out if they do not appear it will look very bad for them.

Those phoning into the incident press room were also furnished with some suggestions as to questions they might ask:

Media – lines that reporters might be taking:

- Why did EWB lend the money in the first place?
- What do EWB feel about the man taking his life?
- Will there be compensation for his mother?
- What checks will be put in place so this doesn't happen again?
- Response to Joe Solomon's comments

- EWB makes so much money and does so at the expense of helpless individuals. How can EWB justify its actions?
- Why does EWB sell costly protection on a loan that couldn't be repaid?

Push for press statement/interview.

- EWB staff – questions from staff
- Staff phoning in to find out the truth about the allegations in the paper
- If questioned by customers, what should they say?
- What checks are put in place to stop inappropriate loans being sold?
- We've been getting calls from the press, what do we say?

Scenario 2. Breaking news

Police have cordoned off the Euro-Wide Bank HQ in London today as a result of what is believed to be a so-called white powder attack.

Members of the emergency services in chemical suits have been seen going into the building on Liverpool Street in the City of London and a decontamination unit is on site.

Police won't say whether a toxic substance has been used or whether anyone has been injured, but no one is allowed in or out of the building.

There is speculation that this is the work of animal rights activists known as the Animal Freedom Movement.

EWB feature on the activists' website as a potential target as they provide loans to Cambridge Life Studies – the company which uses animals as part of its testing procedure.

In the last few minutes the AFM have posted a statement on their website claiming responsibility for the attack:

'Today we have sent a clear message to all those who have connec-
tions with Cambridge Life Studies – that disgusting organization that
abuses animals.

We will attack anyone who profits from the misery and exploitation
of fellow creatures. This is all part of our ongoing campaign.

We know all about the other banks that help Cambridge Life Studies
– we know who you are and your names are on our website.

We never give in and we always win.'

The Euro-Wide Bank is yet to comment, but this must be having a
severe impact on their ability to run their business.

Injections to be used during the course of play:

Scenario 2, Injection 1

The Animal Freedom Movement has just issued a demand on their website
that EWB cease trading for 24 hours from midnight tonight. If they do not a
further chemical attack is planned on another, unspecified EWB building.

Scenario 2, Injection 2

Rumours are circulating that a package containing white powder has been
found at the EWB branch at Jackson Street in Newcastle. Some witnesses are
saying this is another attack – the police are yet to comment.

******

This injection should be used by journalists and members of EWB staff at the
Jackson Street branch.

Scenario 2, Injection 3

There are reports of two members of EWB staff at St Andrew's Square being taken ill. There is immediate speculation that this is as a result of toxic chemical poisoning; some are saying it might be anthrax.

However, another cause may be the severe flu that has been affecting staff recently.

Suggested questions:

Media – lines that reporters might be taking:

- Why is EWB being attacked?
- What is the current situation?
- Are there any injuries/casualties?
- What is EWB's connection with Cambridge Life Studies?
- Security? Security lapse?
- Warnings given?
- Seriousness of attack/chemical?
- Previous threats?
- Effect on business/share price?
- Blackmail?
- Push for press statement/interview.

EWB staff – participants can play the roles of staff or family members of staff phoning in to find out:

- What's going on?
- Are people injured?
- What should they do/where should they go?
- We've been getting calls from the press – what do we say?
- What do we say to customers?
- What about security at our branch?
- Is our ability to trade damaged?
- Should we go to work today?

How the teams fared

Prior to the event, participants were given an overview as to what was expected of them. Facilitators then outlined the running of the exercise.

The teams took a few minutes to find their feet, but most quickly established roles and responsibilities leading to strong team cohesion.

Subsequent analysis of the press statements and briefing notes produced by the teams reflected a strong sense of corporate identity and given that the press love to play divide and rule, this resulted in consistent messages from most teams.

Some players felt that internal communications were handled well whereas some felt that too little information was given to the media.

Those who had to face the television camera towards the end of the exercise found it daunting, but as they were well briefed and had decided on messages they wanted to convey, all gave a credible performance.

From the players' evaluation forms it was clear they felt challenged and engaged throughout the exercise.

Action plan

The feedback from the players and observations from the facilitators informed the report and action plan to further strengthen EWB's communications capability.

I want to stage a similar exercise. Is there anything else I need to know?

The news scenarios are key elements to this type of exercise. For maximum impact, make sure the organization involved is either to blame for something or either rightly or wrongly perceived to be to blame. This will allow for rigorous questioning from the press given that we now live in a blame culture.

- An exercise of this type will either be run by or in conjunction with a senior press officer. If it is the latter make sure you work with them on the planning – particularly on creating and writing the news scenarios
- Keep the participants focused and don't let the timetable slip. Ensure you have enough facilitators to move the teams promptly from one scenario to the next

- Prepare evaluation forms and insist they are completed
- Bring all the participants together at the completion of the exercise and get a spokesperson from each team to talk for no more than five minutes on how their team fared
- If the exercise takes place in the morning remember to provide everyone lunch. They will be tired and hungry!

What have I learnt from this chapter?

- Exercising and training are not one and the same
- Exercise categories reflect the scale of involvement and planning effort required
- The type of exercise chosen will be driven by its aims and objectives
- High-level management endorsement of all aspects of the exercise is essential.

---

3. Planning the exercise

'The best executive is the one who has sense enough to pick good men to do what he wants done, and self-restraint enough to keep from meddling with them while they do it'. Theodore Roosevelt

Getting started

The previous chapter looked at a portfolio of exercise types and showed the importance of setting aims and objectives to help choose the right type of exercise for your needs.

We now look at concepts, tools, and techniques that will provide you with a methodology to help plan your event.

The following planning concepts are infinitely flexible and can be scaled up or down to suit the type of exercise you have in mind.

Exercise planning group

In Chapter 1 we looked at the EPMT. We now turn our attention to the exercise planning group (EPG) who are responsible for the development and delivery of an individual exercise.

Team members will confirm the exercise's aims and objectives, develop the scenario, oversee logistics, deliver the exercise and complete the final report.

One of the first tasks is to decide the make up of the planning group and apportion roles and responsibilities. Roles may include lead planner, support analyst, media adviser and scenario cell manager.

If an exercise is extremely complex, the planning group may be divided into the scenario development team and the logistics team.

Scenario and logistical development are covered in more detail later in this chapter.

Scoping the exercise

Effective scoping, at the outset, will provide direction and guidance during the planning phase.

The scoping process should consider the following:

- The aims and objectives of the exercise
- Outline scenario
- Who will participate in the exercise?
- Type of exercise to be used
- Delivery date(s).

Setting the aims and objectives

The aims and objectives of an exercise are inextricably linked, but must be carefully defined in the planning stage.

Once set, they provide the overarching guidance that informs the development of the exercise. They become the reference point for the final report and will largely determine if the exercise is a success. They will be brought to bear when discussing the type of exercise, who the participants will be and very importantly what scenario should be selected.

Endorsement for the aims and objectives, once they are defined, should be sorted from senior management or the project sponsor.

Outline scenario

A plausible and realistic scenario will not only engage the players, it will also ensure aims and objectives are achieved.

The process of selecting a scenario will be determined by the host of impacts that need to be generated during the course of the event; but bear in mind that the scenario is a vehicle, which drives exercise play. It should never become the focus of the exercise.

When developing an outline scenario, tasks expected of players will be determined by scenario impacts.

The tasks could be decision making or effective media management, while the scenario impacts that trigger the tasks could be denial of access to buildings, closure of a factory or staff absenteeism.

Once the tasks and impacts have been established a scenario should start to emerge – for example, a terror attack, pandemic flu or food contamination.

A simplified diagram of this process can be found in Figure 3.1.

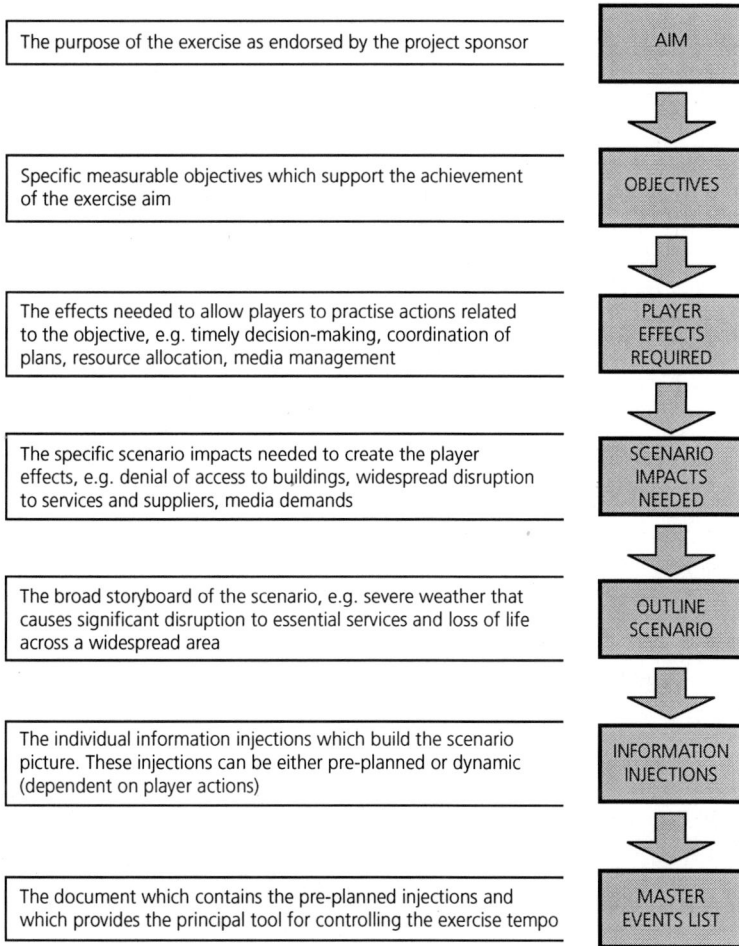

The purpose of the exercise as endorsed by the project sponsor	**AIM**
Specific measurable objectives which support the achievement of the exercise aim	**OBJECTIVES**
The effects needed to allow players to practise actions related to the objective, e.g. timely decision-making, coordination of plans, resource allocation, media management	**PLAYER EFFECTS REQUIRED**
The specific scenario impacts needed to create the player effects, e.g. denial of access to buildings, widespread disruption to services and suppliers, media demands	**SCENARIO IMPACTS NEEDED**
The broad storyboard of the scenario, e.g. severe weather that causes significant disruption to essential services and loss of life across a widespread area	**OUTLINE SCENARIO**
The individual information injections which build the scenario picture. These injections can be either pre-planned or dynamic (dependent on player actions)	**INFORMATION INJECTIONS**
The document which contains the pre-planned injections and which provides the principal tool for controlling the exercise tempo	**MASTER EVENTS LIST**

Figure 3.1

Exercise participation

The two main groups involved in an exercise will be the players and those delivering the event. The latter may include the scenario cell manager, the exercise director and facilitators.

During a simple exercise a facilitator will provide both a 'start state' scenario and questions around which discussions are based.

In most complex and medium exercises players will be likely to respond to an unfolding scenario, with questions and updated information coming from a scenario cell.

The scenario cell is the group that delivers scenario injections to the team or teams being exercised. Injections are constantly updated pieces of information or questions that are fed to the players. A MEL is the complete list of injections used by the scenario cell. The scenario cell will be covered in more detail later in this chapter.

The amount of stakeholders involved in an exercise will vary, depending on its size. A generic list will look something like this:

- Exercise planning group
- Scenario cell
- Scenario cell manager
- Players
- Facilitators
- Observers
- Exercise director
- Scenario experts
- Auditors
- Shareholders
- Industry/industry bodies (associations)
- Board members/directors.

Type of exercise

Choosing the right type of exercise was covered extensively in the previous chapter, but in general terms, simple exercises provide a forum for starting the planning process or for validating plans, while medium and complex exercises are used to test teams in progressively more challenging environments.

As we have seen, choosing the right type of exercise will prove critical to the success of your event.

Delivery dates

The choice of dates for the delivery of an exercise is often determined by participants' availability. However, deputies can be employed, as once an exercise's planning is complete, delay is unwise. Enthusiasm can dissipate and others may become unavailable. Impress upon the participants the need to stick to the original dates laid out in the planning documents.

Exercise specification document

Once the scoping phase has been completed, the exercise specification can be written. This will include decisions made by the exercise planning group, the planning timeline and responsibilities of individuals and teams.

It will also specify the critical documents that need to be produced and delivered. For an example of a completed exercise specification document, please see the case study at the end of this chapter.

Scenario development

When developing a scenario, remember the process as discussed above under 'Outline scenario'. The scenario, let's say pandemic flu, triggers the scenario impacts, e.g. absenteeism, which in turn trigger the tasks the players have to perform – so that the objectives of the exercise can be met.

To guarantee a realistic scenario, specialists can be used to great effect. If a fire is involved, consult the fire service to make sure the details are correct. If the scenario is based around computer failure, consult your IT department to make sure your scenario is plausible.

The scenario development team should meet on a regular basis to coordinate themes and injections.

Developing the MEL

The scenario development team creates the injections that populate the MEL. They do this by analysing the themes contained in the scenario and understanding the impacts on their area of responsibility.

This is how a team member should create an injection:

- Have a general understanding of the scenario
- Understand how the scenario impacts your area of responsibility
- Understand the implications of the impacts on you or your team
- Consider who would tell whom about these impacts.

Table 3.1 shows an example of the injection creation process.

Table 3.1

Overview	Response	Remarks
An understanding of the overall scenario	The 6th floor is on fire @ 9.00 a.m.	
Understand how the scenario impacts on my area of responsibility	1. My team and I work on the 6th floor. 2. My team will all be in work at this time. 3. We will all be evacuated from the building and go to the muster point. No equipment would come out with us. 4. We will not be able to work.	
What are the implications of the impacts for my area of responsibility?	1. Our work is of critical importance to the business. If we do not have models out by 10.00 a.m each morning the business could be fined. 2. We link to Operations. If we don't do our work, they will not be able to do theirs.	1. The regulator would need to be informed.
Consider who would tell whom about the implication and impact and by what method	1. I, Jim Bridges, would inform Toby Mellor that we would not be able to work. 2. Rachel Vickers would call Sonny Parker to tell him that we would not be able to hit our deadlines.	1. They should call CEO and CFO – these individuals are not playing in the exercise.

This process must be conducted for every theme contained in the scenario as it develops. The reason for this is that some interdependencies will be identified and the impact and implications of these will need to be considered.

Each injection is then added to the master events list; an example of part of a MEL is shown in Table 3.2.

The MEL is scalable and may be as simple as five to ten injections from one source, or can contain over three hundred from over fifty sources.

The MEL has many different uses:

- It maintains control of the scenario development
- It controls the exercise tempo
- It holds all the injections
- It identifies the injection delivery mechanisms.

As we have seen, the MEL is split into numerous columns that hold information. Let's look at the critical components:

- Serial – this is the injection number
- Real time – this is the time at which an event or injection occurs. It is classed as 'real time' because the scenario may assume a different 'exercise time' or may involve time jumps
- Exercise time – this is the time at which the scenario is being run, e.g. 'real time' might be 13.00 but 'exercise time' might be 09.00
- From – this is the department or organization from where the injection originates, e.g. IT control room, police
- To – this is where the injection is delivered, e.g. the incident management team/the press room
- By – this is the person, in the scenario cell, who delivers the injection
- Mechanism – this is how the injection is delivered, e.g. phone, email, fax
- Information – this is the information contained in the injection that the player will be given, e.g. 'there is a fire on the 6th floor'
- Remarks – this column contains any additional information relating to the exercise, e.g. 'participants should release a media statement now'.

There is a direct link between the information contained in the MEL and the logistics team. The most important of which is in the delivery mechanism. It is up to the scenario development team to choose the most suitable and realistic method of delivering an injection, but logistics have to provide the means, whether it be phone, fax, email or carrier pigeon.

Planning the exercise

Table 3.2

Serial	Real Time	Exercise Time	From	To	By	Mechanism	Input	Remarks
1	1.00 p.m	8.30 a.m	Security	Gold	Andy	Phone	The 6th floor is on fire	IMT should activate the incident management plan
2	1.01 p.m	8.31 a.m	News One	All	Andy	Website	We are getting breaking news that the 6th floor of that building is on fire	Comms team should report this to the incident management team
3	1.02 p.m	8.32 a.m	The Times	Comms	Jean	Phone	Any casualties? Are your staff all accounted for?	

Enhancing the player experience

The enhancement of a scenario is important as it can bring an exercise to life. The following are recommended:

- News and market data websites
- Video news reports (see case studies for script examples)
- Simulated press conferences
- Using 'real world' communication tools (typically as part of a complex exercise)
- Involving actors or other role players to represent official bodies
- Invite suppliers/customers to take part and respond.

Don't forget: there is no point adding these exercise enhancements if they don't support the aims and objectives of your exercise.

Administration and logistics

In a medium or complex exercise it may be necessary to establish an administration and logistics team. Exercise coordination activities can include:

- Exercise briefings and other communications
- Diary planning and meetings
- Documentation control/quality assurance/budget control
- Command and control preparation
- Communication plans.

Aside from coordinating meetings, and being responsible for the delivery mechanism of the injections provided by the scenario cell, logistics are responsible for the location of the exercise. Rooms used must be large enough to hold all the participants, must contain all the necessary technology such as telephones, computers and fax machines and must be booked well in advance. A recce, by members of the team, the day before the exercise is strongly advised.

Thus logistical and administration resources can include the following:

- Facilities – buildings/rooms
- Refreshments
- Computers (internet capabilities and firewalls)
- Printers
- Stationery

- Projector and screen
- Travel and accommodation (including visas)
- Security clearance
- Communications equipment – phones/fax/email.

Exercise briefings and participant instructions

Exercise briefings are used to explain to participants the aim of the exercise, what their role is within it, what they need do and when and where they are required.

As a guide, initial briefings should be issued a month prior to the exercise, with a reminder sent a week before the exercise delivery date.

Participants should be required to confirm they have received these documents.

Day of delivery briefings are covered extensively in the next chapter.

Diary planning and meetings

The logistics team will coordinate the development and delivery of the exercise. It is up to them to make sure people are available for meetings and that they attend. Individuals with a persuasive demeanour and a sense of humour are invaluable in this role.

They also establish the date of the exercise and the dates, times and venues of all other meetings. Agenda and minutes are also released through the logistics team.

Command and control preparation

It is the responsibility of the logistics team to identify the command and control organization for use during an exercise. In the simple category this may involve just one or two facilitators. However, for a medium or complex exercise there will be many more. Here are some examples:

- **Exercise director** – responsible for the entire exercise – including tempo, control and finish
- **Facilitators** – responsible for their team – they report to the exercise director
- **Scenario cell** – replicates the 'real world' for the players. It delivers information, held in the MEL, to the players and responds to the players'

information requests. Normally made up from members of the scenario development team

- **Control cell**
  - **Logistics cell** – provides logistical support for all participants during the exercise
  - **Call centre** – for use by facilitators to report issues and concerns.

A control cell is only likely to feature in a large-scale exercise.

The scenario cell

The scenario cell replicates the 'real world' and performs a number of tasks:

- Delivers injections to the players
- Stops scenario leakage to non-participants
- Controls the tempo and format of the exercise
- Provides a means of auditing responses and decisions made by participants
- Confirms that communication releases are consistent
- Provides a collective group of experts to create new injections as they become necessary.

The scenario development team normally populates the scenario cell. They are experts in their field, have been involved in the planning process and can respond credibly to player requests.

Scenario cell members are isolated from the players, typically delivering their injections by phone, fax or email. In a large exercise, extra individuals can be drafted into this team to provide a call centre or to increase the number of injections, should it be deemed necessary by the scenario cell manager or the exercise director.

The scenario cell manager must make sure all injections are delivered on time and can make changes and amendments to the scenario as required, but always in consultation with the exercise director.

Communication plan

During the preparation of an exercise there will be a considerable amount of communication between members of the exercise planning group and others.

Understanding who will receive what information and when is complex. Because of this, communication plans should be established:

- Pre- and post-exercise communication plan
- Exercise communications plan.

The pre- and post-exercise communication plan is established to coordinate the planning of the exercise and management of exercise learning. Table 3.3 shows the general detail required for each of the plans and some example subjects.

Table 3.3

Type	Aim	Plan	Example Subjects
Pre- and post- exercise communication plan	To provide effective communication to exercise participants in order to coordinate the exercise planning process and management of the lessons learnt	1. Communication recipients • Media • Players • Logistic team members • Scenario cell members • Command and control members • Stakeholders 2. Methods of communicating 3. Frequency of communications	1. Exercise Introduction 2. Health & Safety requirements 3. Exercise contacts directory 4. Proposal paper 5. Outline dates 6. Cost estimates 7. Exercise management structure 8. Exercise communiqués 9. Feedback 10. Reports
Exercise communication plan	To provide clear guidance to exercise participants, including contact details, in order that everybody involved in the exercise knows who and when to communicate with	1. Player structure including contact details 2. Command and control including contact details	1. Delivery mechanisms 2. Telephone directories 3. Exercise log 4. Intranet/Internet pages and usernames/ passwords

Final thoughts

Even simple exercises require a great deal of planning. However, once the master events list is in place, briefings have been sent to all participants and rooms where the event will take place have been booked, the planning phase is complete.

If all elements of this chapter are in place, there is every reason to believe that when delivery day arrives, the exercise will get off to a brisk and compelling start.

Case study

In this case study we look at actual materials used in the development and delivery of a simple exercise. For the purpose of this book the company involved is Merryweather plc.

Producing an exercise specification document is a major milestone in the development of an exercise. We looked at its component parts in Chapter 1. We now want to show you how the parts go together to form a complete document.

Exercise specification

Aim

The aim of the desktop exercise is to introduce incident management to Merryweather's board in order to provide an opportunity to develop an incident management plan.

Specific objectives

- To introduce incident management characteristics, principles and tools to Merryweather
- To discuss and agree a suitable incident management plan and organization
- To discuss and agree suitable incident management policies, procedures and processes
- To discuss and agree suitable administration and logistical support for an incident management plan.

Participants

The following individuals will attend and be divided into two teams:

Team A – incident management team
Team B – CEO and other senior executives.

Structure

The desktop exercise will split into three phases:

1. Introduction to incident management, characteristics, principles and tools
2. Three scenario discussions forums
3. Debrief.

Format

The desktop exercise phases will be conducted as follows:

Phase 1

- Group presentation

Phase 2 – Scenario format

- 5 minute scenario presentation
- 30 minute scenario discussion
- 15 minute back briefs and discussion

Phase 3

- Group discussion.

Scenario

Merryweather is requested to pick three of the following four scenarios for use during the desktop exercise. Once decided, a detailed scenario document will be drafted. Final details will be compiled during the scenario development meeting.

Scenario 1

Fire at Merryweather's Birmingham offices. The building is evacuated and power cut off by the fire service. There is some damage to the premises.

Scenario 2

IT network failure. Details will be finalized during the scenario development meeting. The aim of this scenario is to disrupt Merryweather's service provision.

Scenario 3

Headquarters evacuated. The building is evacuated on orders from the police. Possible vehicle crash, gas leak – details to be confirmed – but an incident over which Merryweather has little control. Building will be sealed off for at least 24 hours.

Scenario 4

Fuel and transport strike. An upcoming, simultaneous fuel and rail strike poses a threat to petrol supply and public transport – all of which will cause mass absenteeism among Merryweather staff.

Desktop exercise timings

The desktop exercise will take place on 17 October – between 9.00 a.m and 1.00 p.m.

Preparation

The recommended preparation time line for this desktop exercise is:

- Week beginning 27 August – confirm scenarios
- Week beginning 10 September – desktop exercise scenario development meeting

Planning the exercise

- Week beginning 24 September – media filming
- Week beginning 1 October – desktop exercise coordination meeting
- 16 October – desktop exercise preparation
- 17 October – desktop exercise
- 26 October – submit desktop exercise report

Table 3.4

Item	Time	Activity	Remarks
16 October			
1	3.00 p.m	Set up and rehearsal	
17 October			
2	8.00 a.m	Delivery team arrive	
3	9.00 to 9.10 a.m	Desktop exercise starts – introduction	
4	9.10 to 9.50 a.m	Introduction to incident management	
5	9.50 to 10.40 a.m	Scenario 1	
6	10.40 to 11.30 a.m	Scenario 2	
7	11.30 to 11.40 a.m	Coffee break	
8	11.40 a.m to 12.30 p.m	Scenario 3	
9	12.30 to 1.00 p.m	Debrief	Desktop exercise ends

Resources

Delivery

The delivery team will consist of the exercise director and two facilitators.

Logistics

The logistics team will provide the following:

- Laptop computer for presentation including loudspeakers and projector
- One large meeting room for presentation to all participants
- One smaller meeting room used by B team when groups divide
- Tea and coffee for arrival and break.

Post desktop exercise

The business continuity team will submit an exercise report containing an action plan within seven working days.

Desktop exercise delivery

We will now look at an aspect of the delivery of the desktop exercise and the materials employed – specifically one of the scenario-based discussions.

To aid their deliberations delegates were provided with a scenario – including background information, emergency services response, maps, Merryweather's position in the scenario together with a video news clip describing the scene.

Participants were to consider themselves to be at their normal place of work and to have use of their usual telecoms and IT equipment.

The teams were given the following 'start state' or background information:

- There is a fire at the car garage next to your Birmingham premises
- The fire started at 9.30 a.m
- Fire service are tackling the blaze
- Police have set up cordons and evacuated buildings
- Electricity in the local area has been switched off

Planning the exercise

- People with serious injuries have been taken to hospital
- Walking wounded being treated by paramedics at the site.

Participants then watched a news broadcast:

> Good morning. We're just getting reports of a serious fire at an industrial estate just off Meadow Street in the Ladywood area of Birmingham.
>
> Eyewitnesses say the blaze started at a garage or bodywork repair shop that may contain plastics, chemicals and gas cylinders – thick smoke is covering the area.
>
> Because of fears of an explosion – police have set up a 200 metre cordon around the estate, which is home to a number of businesses including Merryweather plc – several have been evacuated.
>
> Ten fire crews are battling the blaze and local electricity supplies have been switched off.
>
> We have no word on casualties but there are unconfirmed reports that police suspect arson could be involved.
>
> We'll bring you more on this story as we get it.

Players were then brought up to date on Merryweather's situation:

- One casualty confirmed – a sales representative – in hospital, but condition unknown
- All staff evacuated from the building and waiting for the all clear from the fire service to re-enter the premises
- Electricity to building cut off
- Fire service say building will be cordoned off until fire is out and area is safe
- Emergency batteries that power the IT server could last anything between an hour and twenty four hours depending on usage
- All Merryweather support centres may lose connectivity – special concern lies with London.

The following questions were crafted to spur discussion.

These for team A – the incident management team:

- Who is responsible for evaluating the situation and activating the incident management team?
- How and by whom would you (individually) expect to be informed of the incident?
- How would you communicate with each other?
- What is your initial meeting agenda?
- Who would chair the meeting and who would record the information, decisions and actions discussed?
- Would you expect anybody else, within the company, to be responding to this incident and how?

These for team B – CEO and senior executives:

- How and by whom would you (individually) expect to be informed of this incident?
- Would you be expecting anybody else to be responding to this incident and how?
- What are you expecting from the incident management team?
- How would you (individually) be informed of any decisions taken by the incident management team?
- How would you coordinate work between each other?

What benefits have I derived from this case study?

- I now know what a completed exercise specification document should look like
- I now understand the importance of a timeline in exercise delivery
- I have a clear idea of what materials are needed to promote a successful desktop exercise discussion
- I understand the importance of devising the right questions to test plans and procedures.

What have I learnt from this chapter?

- How to scope an exercise
- How to develop a scenario
- The importance of the scenario cell
- The role of the master events list
- How to enhance an exercise
- How to develop a command and control organization.

4. Delivering the exercise

'Next week there can't be any crisis. My schedule is already full'. Henry A. Kissinger

The importance of an effective start

All the planning and development has been done and the day of the exercise has finally arrived.

For many people taking part this will be their first experience of such an event. Quite naturally some will feel apprehensive or may well have pressing work they will inevitably believe is more important. A slick, seamless and good-humoured start is the best way to engage and enthuse all participants.

Players should have been sent a briefing document (participant's instructions), which will tell them where they have to be and what they might have to read or bring with them.

For participants to start the exercise in a positive frame of mind, they must be given as much information as possible – this will be achieved through preparation and briefing.

It must be effectively conveyed that those who have devised and planned the exercise and are in control of the event are keen to make it a success and believe that it will bring benefits to all involved. Facilitators must make clear the exercise is not a test of individuals, but rather an opportunity to test plans and procedures.

If players sense this and if the exercise gets off to a brisk and engaging start, many of their fears will evaporate as they become involved in the event and find themselves enjoying it.

Final preparations

Ideally the final preparations for the exercise should be completed the day before and checked again two hours prior to the start.

The following checklist will prove useful for all types of exercise:

- Do all participants have access to the building(s)?
- If passes are required, have they been provided?

Delivering the exercise

- Is the room(s) suitable for those taking part?
- Are there sufficient chairs and tables?
- Are there sufficient wall clocks? (Especially relevant if 'exercise time' is being used)
- Do they work?
- Are there sufficient PowerPoint slides?
- Are the projection facilities adequate?
- Have they been tested?
- Are alternative arrangements in place?
- Have they been tested?
- Are the video/DVD/audio facilities adequate?
- Have they been tested?
- Are alternative arrangements in place?
- Are there sufficient copies of audio tapes, videos and DVDs?
- Has sufficient stationery been provided (pens, pencils, paper)?
- Are there sufficient white boards, flip charts?
- Are there sufficient markers/rubbers for white boards, flip charts?
- Are there sufficient PCs for internet access?
- Have they been tested?
- Can exercise websites be accessed?
- Are there sufficient telephones?
- Are there sufficient spider telephones?
- Have they all been tested and the numbers checked against the exercise telephone directory?
- If mobile phones are being used, is the network signal sufficiently robust and are the phones fully charged?
- Have they all been tested and the numbers checked against the exercise telephone directory?
- Are the numbers and access codes for audio conference calls correct?
- Have they been tested and the numbers checked against the exercise telephone directory?
- Are there sufficient fax facilities?
- Have they been tested and the numbers checked against the exercise telephone directory?
- Are there sufficient video conference facilities?
- Have they all been tested?

- If exercise email is used are all the addresses correct?
- Has it been tested and the addresses checked against the exercise telephone directory?
- Are contingency communications in place?
- Have they been sufficiently widely promulgated?
- Have they been tested?
- Are there sufficient copies of the master events list?
- Are there sufficient copies of the exercise telephone directory?
- Are there sufficient copies of the red, amber, green traffic light report criteria? (See Chapter 5 which looks at the traffic light system of reporting)
- Are there sufficient copies of participant feedback forms?
- Are there sufficient copies of any other exercise documentation (player briefs, facilitator briefs etc.)?
- Have sufficient refreshments been ordered?
- Are there arrangements in place for visitors or observers?

It must be borne in mind that this is not an exhaustive list as different types of exercises, different types of locations, different numbers of players and facilitators and different methods of communication will generate unique requirements. However, the bottom line is that every aspect of delivering the exercise must be questioned, checked and tested – and then questioned, checked and tested again. Nothing must be left to chance.

Remember the 5 Ps: *Prior Preparation Prevents Poor Performance.*

Players' briefing

All final preparations must be completed well before participants arrive for the exercise.

Facilitators should be on hand to meet and greet their teams, explain the layout of the room and answer any last minute questions. The aim is to engender a relaxed atmosphere, which creates an eager anticipation of the event. An unfriendly, disorganized welcome is likely to mean a loss of attention and enthusiasm among the players – essential mindsets that could prove hard to regain.

The exercise will start with a briefing to the players. Not all teams may be at the same location and in this case it is important to ensure that the same brief is given at all player locations at the same time.

Delivering the exercise

A PowerPoint presentation is an effective delivery mechanism for the player brief. If it is well presented, it immediately introduces a professional and efficient tone for the day. The brief should be tailored to suit the players dependent on their experience and the type of exercise. It should last no more than fifteen minutes but contain all the information the players need to engage fully in the 'virtual world' they are about to inhabit.

Different exercises will require different information but the following should prove useful when preparing a presentation:

- Why they are participating in the exercise?
- Who else is participating in the exercise?
- The purpose of the exercise
- The exercise objectives
- The overall time line of the exercise
- Their role in the exercise
- How the 'virtual world' will be created and the importance that, for the duration of the exercise, they divorce themselves from the 'real world'
- The role and composition of the scenario cell
- Communications that may be used
- Communications that may not be used (turn off personal mobile phones, Blackberries, pagers unless being used in the exercise)
- Explain the use of the exercise telephone directory
- Explain the use of other inputs such as video footage, audio recordings, exercise websites, exercise email, exercise fax
- If all the players are briefed centrally, introduce the facilitators and explain their role
- Stress the testing of plans and procedures, not the testing of individuals
- Ask for their cooperation in accepting the scenario without question – it is merely a vehicle to achieve the objectives
- Ask for their acceptance of any known exercise artificialities
- Ask for their full engagement as this will produce a more meaningful, useful and enjoyable exercise
- Explain debrief and feedback arrangements
- When refreshments will be provided
- The presence of any visitors or observers
- Final questions.

Executive briefing

The exercise may involve senior executives who will require a separate briefing on their participation. This is to be welcomed and presents an ideal opportunity to engage senior management in business continuity and lead them to a greater understanding of the importance of exercising plans, procedures and people. They might not participate in the whole event so it is important that the exercise is designed to maximize their involvement and that any briefing given is succinct and relevant to them.

A good way to approach the briefing is to ask yourself, if I were the senior executive, what are the key points I need to know and what will be expected of me? Senior executives will not thank you if they are caught out or embarrassed because the briefing was inadequate or if they believe you are wasting their time with trivial detail. Much will depend on the personality of the senior executive and what they know of the exercise, but the following should certainly be covered:

- Exercise aims and objectives
- Exercise locations – those relevant to the senior executive
- Exercise timings – when the senior executive should arrive and when they will be free to leave
- Outline of who is participating in the exercise
- Detail of exactly what role is expected of them, who they will be able to call on for support and who they may have to report to
- Any specific exercise requirements that will impact them directly
- An exercise debrief that they may be invited to chair
- Any documentation they should have read or brought with them
- The presence of any visitors or observers
- Any questions they may have.

Facilitator briefing

It is standard practice to have a facilitator with each team being exercised but it is likely that not all facilitators will have been involved in the planning process. In addition they could come from business areas outside those involved in the exercise and may know little about these departments. However, it is essential that all facilitators are fully conversant with the exercise and their role within it.

Delivering the exercise

Ideally, two weeks prior to the event, all facilitators should be given brief details of where they have to be and when – together with an outline of the exercise objectives, scenario and which team they will be facilitating.

The role of a facilitator will vary depending on the nature of the exercise. In simple exercises designed to challenge plans and procedures, the facilitator may be required to lead or steer discussions to ensure specific issues are fully explored.

In medium and complex exercises the role of the facilitator is more of an observer, noting how the team functioned, resolving conflicts and offering advice. Their role is also to ensure the exercise does not stray beyond its boundaries and to monitor its progress.

The day before the exercise the facilitators should receive a verbal briefing from the exercise planner. This should cover the following points:

- Brief introduction to the business areas being exercised
- Brief introduction to the incident management structure
- Exercise purpose
- Exercise objectives
- Outline scenario
- Copy of the final master events list
- Copy of the final exercise telephone directory
- Which teams, or specific individuals are participating as players
- Which teams they are to facilitate
- Their role as a facilitator
- Communications to be used by the players
- Communications to be used by the facilitators
- Requirement for and use of laptops, PCs, internet, email, exercise websites, video footage, audio tapes, telephones
- Requirement for verbal briefings to the players
- Any specific actions during the exercise
- Any specific issues to track during the exercise
- Data collection for post exercise reporting
- Post exercise hot debrief
- Arrangements for refreshments.

Scenario cell manager

Ideally the scenario cell manager (SCM) should be involved in the planning of the exercise from the very beginning so that he or she has an in-depth understanding of the background to the scenario and how the exercise objectives will be achieved.

The most important part of the planning process, from the SCM's perspective, is the creation of the MEL. To that end, they should chair all scenario cell meetings while the MEL is being populated. Thereafter, the SCM becomes the auditor in chief of the MEL so that on the day of the exercise, they have a detailed and intimate knowledge of its content, understanding fully the impact of each injection and the expected responses.

If, for whatever reason, the SCM has not been involved in the planning process, it is absolutely essential that they study the MEL in great detail as far in advance of the exercise as possible.

On the day of the exercise, the SCM is responsible for carrying out all the final preparations listed above as far as they apply to the scenario cell. Lastly, the scenario cell must be briefed.

Scenario cell: briefing and final checks

A good relationship with the members of the scenario cell should have already been established during the scenario planning meetings. However, it is possible that some members may not have been involved in the planning process, so it is important that everyone is thoroughly briefed on their role and responsibilities for the day.

The scenario cell should assemble in their designated room at least 30 minutes before the exercise starts. The following checklist should then be used to ensure the scenario cell is, in every respect, ready to deliver the exercise:

- Check there is a white board or flip chart for recording key information, decisions and milestones during the exercise. This is important as it provides all members of the scenario cell with an overview of the progress of the exercise as a whole. In an intensive exercise it is easy for members to become immersed in their own area and not be aware of decisions that have been taken that might have a bearing on future injections

Delivering the exercise

- Check there is a master clock that all can see. The MEL will have been written with specific injections being made at specific times to generate the required response. It is therefore imperative that all involved in the exercise work to exactly the same time. Hence the importance of the master clock. In exercises where the 'exercise time' is different to 'real time', the clock must show the 'exercise time'. This will help the team (and players) immerse themselves in the scenario. There must be no confusion as to what times are being used
- Check that all those expected in the scenario cell are actually present. If any have not been part of the team which produced the MEL, be prepared to brief them on the overall scenario and their part in it. If members are missing, reallocate the injections they were responsible for delivering to other, named members
- Check all have the latest MEL. During the planning process, many different versions of the MEL will have been produced but all those delivering the exercise, including facilitators, must work from the final, agreed version. To that end, ensure spare copies are available for distribution if required
- Brief the exercise start and finish times to ensure that all members are in no doubt as to how long they will be required
- Ensure sufficient copies of the final version of the exercise telephone directory are available. Like the MEL, the exercise telephone directory will have gone through various versions and will probably be the last exercise document to be produced. Ensure that all members understand the exercise telephone directory and how they make contact with the players
- Ensure all scenario cell members know the numbers for which they are responsible and who could and should answer calls to numbers that have been allocated to 'other' (for example contractors or the emergency services) as opposed to specific business areas
- Brief the team on their role and how to deliver the injections
- To the players, you alone represent the outside world. This includes all the Business Areas represented but could also be anyone else the players wish to contact. You should be prepared for impromptu role-play
- Before delivering an injection, read what you are about to say and try to get into character
- When delivering an injection, call the person using the number in the Exercise Telephone Directory, ask for that person or, if they are unavailable, ask to leave a message. If asked, or required, give your name and your exercise phone number

- The injection as it appears in the MEL may be a scripted message or just an outline of key information. When delivering it, you do not have to read it verbatim. What is important is that the key information it contains is clearly conveyed. Be creative and natural but be careful not to impart anything that is not in the written injection as this could lead to later confusion or introduce an issue that might detract from the overall scenario
- Some players might try to 'fight' the scenario or the thrust of what you are saying. In this case, do not get into an argument, stay in character, repeat the information, ensure it has been received and hang up
- If you receive a call, ascertain who is calling, who they want to talk to and the subject matter. If you can deal with the issue do so. If not, either pass the call to someone who can or say that you will call them back later. It is entirely realistic not to answer all questions immediately. Note what was said and if necessary ensure it is put on the white board/flip chart. If you have said you will call back later, do not forget to do so
- During some exercises it may have been decided that each injection is prefaced with 'This is part of the exercise ...' so as to make clear it is not a 'real world' event. If this device is being used, scenario cell members must be told
- If web pages, video footage or radio broadcasts are being employed during the exercise, they should be made available to the scenario cell. This not only helps to integrate the team into the exercise but it ensures that they see and hear the same information that the players are being given. As part of the room set-up it is therefore essential to check that any equipment needed to display this information is both present and works
- It is important that the scenario cell focuses fully on the exercise and they should be asked to turn off their personal mobile phones, Blackberries and pagers during the exercise. If for operational reasons, this is not possible, they should be asked to leave the room when answering non-exercise calls
- For the comfort and safety of the scenario team, evacuation procedures should be briefed. In addition, the location of toilets and any arrangements that might have been made for refreshments should also be given
- Lastly, it is important that the team approach their task with enthusiasm as this will feed through to the players and add to the realism of the scenario. The team should therefore be given every encouragement to enjoy the role they are about to play.

Visitors and observers

Various people may want to observe the exercise. Who they are must be ascertained well in advance as, like everything else, preparations will have to be made for their visit. All visitors and observers must be approved, but check this has been done, as people turning up unannounced can be very distracting. Visitors must have a valid reason for being there and must not get in the way.

Incident simulations can be high-pressure events, so it is essential that visitors do not interfere in the exercise and that their presence does not put any added pressure on the players. Players and executives should be made aware of who is visiting and why.

Depending on the reason for the visit, the person nominated to escort the visitors should be prepared to brief them on the scenario, the exercise objectives, how the exercise will be controlled, the scenario cell, and what is expected of the players. Unless cleared to do so, they should not take any exercise documentation away with them.

During the exercise

Simple exercises

For facilitated discussions it is not enough to present a situation and expect everyone to start talking. The sessions have to be structured to achieve the desired results. Free flowing discussions can soon degenerate into arguments or stray widely from the intended issues.

It is therefore important to know exactly how you want the discussions to progress and to keep them on track without seeming to dominate. Using the exercise objectives it should be possible to script questions that address the issues. They need not all be used but will assist in steering talks in the required direction.

For example, if an exercise objective is to examine the roles and responsibilities of team members, a specific issue could be the initial activation of the BCP and assembling the incident management team. In this case questions such as the following should be prepared:

- Who is in the incident team?
- Are all aspects of the business represented?
- Are the roles and responsibilities clearly defined and understood?

- Who authorizes their activation?
- Where does the incident team assemble? Who decides? How are they told?
- How long will it all take? What do they take with them?
- How are staff not yet at work contacted?
- Is there a call cascade system? Is it up to date?
- Who informs higher chain of command? How is it done? Are there criteria for doing so?
- What if it is out of working hours?
- How do you gain access to offices/buildings out of hours?
- Where do staff go?
- Who looks after them?
- Who accounts for them?
- What if not all can be accounted for?
- What if there are casualties?

For the communications team, the following is suggested:

- How would you expect to communicate with your people?
- What if it is out of working hours?
- Do you talk to the media? If yes, what message should be given out? Who signs off on what goes to media and staff?
- Do you have pre-prepared statements?
- When and how often would you communicate with the higher chain of command? Are there standard situation reports?
- How do you communicate with clients? At what stage? What message do you give?
- How do you ensure a common approach to what is said to all stakeholders, so there is a clarity and consistency of message?

For information gathering and management teams, the following is suggested:

- What information do you need and who will provide it?
- How do you assess the impact on the business?
- How is this information used – collated, analysed, recorded?

For decision-making teams, the following is suggested:

- What is the current known impact – on business, on people?
- What is the overall aim, the desired end state?

- What are the immediate actions, priorities?
- What is the most important action to take right now?
- What is needed to achieve the immediate actions?
- How is a coordinated response achieved?
- What decisions are the team empowered to make?

The facilitator must keep the discussions flowing and must never raise questions that only require a yes or no answer.

For more information on delivering a simple exercise see the case study in Chapter 3.

Above all, the facilitator must be receptive to what is being said and be adaptable as it is quite likely that participants will introduce unexpected, but valid suggestions. Indeed, in many respects, this is one of the reasons for conducting such an event.

And remember: some participants will dominate the conversation whereas others, with plenty of good ideas, may need to be encouraged.

An eye must be kept on the clock to ensure that all the required outcomes of the exercise can be adequately covered in the time allotted.

Medium exercises

In most medium and complex exercises, the scenario cell is the engine room and the scenario cell manager is the chief engineer. If the MEL is well written, all the preparations completed and everyone fully briefed, there may be a perception that the exercise will run itself. On a few occasions this might be the case but the secret and indeed strength of a simulation exercise is that it must be dynamic. It must be able to react to players' actions, which may not have been anticipated.

A key element in making the exercise dynamic is good communication between the exercise director, the facilitators and scenario cell manager. The facilitators must be able to recognize if a team is getting overloaded or is under engaged and communicate this to the scenario cell manager. He or she must then decide which injections to remove or which extra injections should be inserted to achieve the required effect.

In a similar vein, the exercise director, the scenario cell manager and facilitators must follow the progress of the responses, requests and decisions made by the players to ensure that forthcoming injections remain valid or new ones are crafted to reflect a changing situation.

A specific example would be an exercise that is expected to lead to a decision to invoke a disaster recovery site. If it becomes clear that the decision is not going to be taken, thereby possibly negating an exercise objective of testing invocation procedures, an injection will have to be inserted to force the decision. Similarly if invocation was decided upon earlier than anticipated, it may well be necessary to amend injections that were concerned with pre-invocation issues.

The key to maintaining the dynamism of the exercise is flexibility. No matter how good the preparations, it is quite likely that something will crop up unexpectedly. It is therefore incumbent on the exercise director, the scenario cell manager and all facilitators to be alert.

Complex exercises

In many respects, the issues involved in delivering a complex exercise will be similar to a medium exercise. Without a doubt the same level of preparation will be required. The main difference will lie in what particular element of realism is introduced thus making it a complex exercise.

For example it might be a 'no notice' activation exercise. If this is the case a briefing to the players will not be required, nor will many of the preparations to create a 'virtual world'. However, the introduction of 'reality' to an exercise brings its own problems.

The main issue is how to contain the realism – how to stop it getting out of control. In this respect it is vital that the exercise 'boundaries' are clearly defined from the outset and are briefed to all facilitators. Do you really want to evacuate your building? Should your incident management team actually go to the disaster recovery site? Are you sure you want to get staff out of bed at 3 a.m?

All these will add reality but can have profound consequences. Will the police be happy to see your staff blocking the pavement outside your offices for no apparent reason? Is the DR site prepared to take your incident management team? How much will this cost?

Another aspect of keeping the exercise within the defined boundaries is how far you let people believe they are involved in a real incident as opposed to an exercise.

You probably want them to react as they would in real life, but when a fire alarm goes off, what happens when someone calls the fire brigade? How do you stop them doing so?

In adversity, people contact their relatives to let them know they are all right. This immediately puts the virtual world into the public domain. How do you control this?

And how long do you expect the exercise to run? One great advantage of a simulated exercise is that all the players start the exercise at the same time and time can be compressed to test various stages of a plan. Not so with reality. If you have allotted three hours for the exercise and, because of traffic, it takes most of the players three hours to get to the disaster recovery site what has been achieved?

It must be appreciated that reality often takes longer than simulation so it must be asked what can reasonably be expected in the timescale.

In any complex exercise the key factors are therefore:

- What am I actually trying to achieve?
- How far am I willing to go?
- How do I stop it going too far?
- How long will it actually take?

Adding real events to an exercise will undoubtedly make them challenging for the players, the planners and those who deliver the event.

Stopping the exercise

In the event of a 'real world' event occurring, which necessitates stopping the exercise, there must be a clearly defined and briefed procedure for doing so. This should include identifying, who has the authority to stop the exercise and how this will be communicated to all participants.

It does happen. Halfway through the UK Government's National Avian Influenza exercise in 2006, a dead swan was discovered which tested positive for the H5N1 virus. The exercise was halted and those involved moved seamlessly from exercise to reality.

Post exercise debrief

When the exercise finishes, this is the moment to capture key learning points while they are still fresh in people's minds. It is therefore advisable to conduct some form of debrief as soon as possible.

For a simple exercise this may take the form of a quick wash-up session to capture what has been discussed. A summary of key points should be given so that participants leave feeling they have made a valued contribution and have learnt something. Better still to identify issues that require specific action.

For medium and complex exercises the debrief should be treated as an event in itself and subject to prior planning.

- It should first be established who will participate in the debrief. Where many players are involved it may not be desirable for them all to attend. Provision should be made for someone to represent the views of those not attending
- Having established who will attend it will be necessary to select a suitable venue. Ideally this should be the location of the exercise but where teams are in more than one location, it may be necessary to delay the start to enable people to travel to the chosen location. Alternatively, debriefs can be held by audio or video conference calls. In this case, these facilities must be checked as part of the exercise preparations mentioned above
- The choice of attendees and locations will partially dictate when the debrief will take place and how long it will last. Ideally it will start as soon after the exercise as possible. The duration may be dictated by the number of participants but 45 minutes is a reasonable planning figure. Whatever is decided must be promulgated well before the exercise so that all participants are aware of the requirements.
- It is also important to establish who will chair the debrief. This could be the exercise director or one of the senior players but whoever it is, it is essential that they know what format the debrief will take
- This format may vary but it is important to have a clear idea of how the debrief will be conducted before it starts – a definite structure is essential
- One example is to invite a spokesperson from each team to give three key observations of:
  1. What went well
  2. What didn't go well
  3. What needs to be done
- Doing this ensures that all the participants are giving their feedback in the same way. Limiting it to three points concentrates the mind and keeps the discussions relatively brief. The observations should concern the plans, procedures and responses, not how the exercise was conducted as this will be covered in the participant's feedback form

- Finally, someone should be nominated to record all that is said. The outcomes of the debrief will almost certainly form part of any final, written report and so it is essential that the key issues are captured at the time.

Participant's feedback form

To give everyone an opportunity to comment on the exercise and to supplement points raised at the debrief, it is useful to invite all participants to complete a feedback questionnaire. These should be prepared in advance and sufficient copies must be made available on the day. If practicable, they should be completed immediately after the exercise. Experience shows that if they are given out and asked to be returned at a later date, few are actually received. To ensure completion by all it is suggested that the participants are asked to hand them in on leaving the room.

The next chapter, on report writing, looks in detail at the importance of capturing player feedback and suggests methods as to how this can be done.

Facilitator's debrief

Just as it is important to capture the players' thoughts immediately after the exercise, so it is important to capture the facilitators' observations. A time and venue for this should be agreed in advance of the exercise. It should be held after the participants' debrief and well away from any of the players.

It is best conducted using the traffic light process, which will be discussed in the following chapter.

Holding the debrief will also assist the person nominated to write the final report to get a feel for the main issues before studying the facilitators' written reports in detail.

Before you go

Most exercises will be commercially sensitive and it is important that no exercise material is left in any of the exercise locations. All rooms used should be completely cleared of any documents, white boards must be wiped clean and flip charts either retained for analysis or destroyed. Given the amount of paperwork involved in an exercise, it is advisable to agree disposal arrangements ahead of time.

Check that DVDs, videos and audio tapes have been removed from machines and that exercise websites and email accounts have been disabled. Finally, make sure that no exercise equipment is left behind.

What have I learnt from this chapter?

- The exercise should take place in an atmosphere which engenders eager anticipation in the players
- The scenario cell manager should be centrally involved in producing the MEL
- A robust communications plan is essential
- The keys to simulation exercise are dynamism and flexibility
- Observations and lessons identified must be captured immediately after the exercise
- Exercise boundaries must be clearly established and measures put in place to remain within them.

Case study

Background

A medium simulation exercise was conducted for a business in the food processing industry – an owner of several factories and premises across the UK. For the purposes of this book the company is called Brighter Meats. The major supermarket chain they supply is LoCost.

A new incident management plan had recently been written as the company wanted to adopt a group approach to incident management. This involved the establishment of gold, silver and bronze incident management teams (see glossary). In addition the exercise was used as a vehicle to test some of the assumptions regarding a major refurbishment project that was being planned at the site chosen for the exercise.

> ### Purpose
>
> To run an exercise that integrates building awareness of the incident management plan while at the same time challenging some component parts of the risk assessments prepared for the refurbishment project.

> ## Specific objectives
>
> - To validate the group incident management plan
> - To develop the incident management team's understanding of the group incident management plan
> - To exercise selected component parts of the refurbishment project risk assessments
> - To develop a creative approach to problem solving.

The exercise was scheduled to take place from 10.00 a.m until 2.00 p.m.

The players

It was decided the exercise would concentrate on the silver team (the incident planners) at one of the processing plants but there was also the desire to involve gold team members (senior executives including the CEO). However, they could not commit to the full timescale of the exercise and it was unlikely that they would all be able to participate from one location.

Building the scenario

The scenario centred on contamination issues, unknowingly caused by a refurbishment project. To gradually increase the complexity of issues and ensure gold team involvement in the later stages only, it was decided to run the exercise in three distinct sessions, each lasting one hour.

Having designed and agreed the outline scenario, a scenario cell of five were chosen who were able to provide expertise on all aspects of the business and the refurbishment. They met two months before the exercise and in the course of the following six weeks, produced a master events list with twelve injections per session. This relatively slow pace provided a good balance between keeping the players engaged by introducing new, significant information and allowing the players sufficient time to consider fully the issues involved.

Preparations

Prior to the exercise all players were sent participant's instructions so they were in no doubt as to where they had to be and what was expected of them.

The silver team, consisting of twelve players, assembled in a room, which was equipped with a flip chart, a television and twelve internal phones.

The scenario cell were in another room also equipped with a flip chart, a television and six internal phones. The use of internal phones ensured the integrity of the 'virtual world' plus mobile phone reception was unreliable.

An added communications problem was how to ensure the participation of the five gold team members who would be playing from their normal places of work. This was solved by providing and promulgating an exercise audio conference call facility, with a back up, which was used for the silver to gold briefings and the gold team discussions, all of which could be monitored by the facilitators and the scenario cell.

During the first 15 minutes, the silver team were briefed on the format of the exercise and the communications protocols. The gold team were given a similar brief via the audio conference call facility 15 minutes before their participation in the exercise. The previous day they had been sent the PowerPoint slides used for the initial briefing so they could view them while being briefed verbally. They were also given details of the scenario up to the point at which their participation started.

The fact that the gold team played from their normal workplace added to the reality of the exercise but also introduced an exercise artificiality. In order for them to view the simulated news broadcasts, they were made available on a password-protected exercise website. Details of how and when to access the website were sent to each of the gold team members the day before the exercise but they were asked not to view the news broadcasts until the appropriate times.

The exercise was run by a scenario cell manager and two other facilitators, one with the silver team and the other monitoring the gold team's discussions. A 'red – amber – green' traffic light report format had been agreed as part of the exercise planning process which identified a comprehensive list of aspects to be benchmarked.

The first session

The first session involved only the silver team and started with a pre-prepared briefing by the silver team leader on what had happened and why they were meeting.

> The day is today, Tuesday 10.15 a.m.
>
> Five weeks ago, the project to refurbish Building A commenced. In the following three weeks numerous wall panels were replaced and a wall knocked through to allow machines to be moved in and out. Three days ago there was a weekend shut down to allow the refurbishment work to progress. New wall and ceiling panels were installed and refrigeration lagging was replaced, as were light fittings and bulbs.
>
> At the same time there was extensive cutting and grinding work on new pipelines as all utility supplies (steam, water, air) were being progressively renewed. In addition various doors were replaced. The contractor commented that all the concurrent work was stretching his resources. On Sunday a hygiene crew came in to the plant to clean and production started at 4.00 a.m the following morning (Monday). During the weekend an upturn in orders reduced stock.

This achieved a definite 'start' to the exercise and engaged the team leader from the outset. The scenario cell delivered injections, which prompted actions to be taken following the discovery of product contamination. There follows some examples as they appeared in the master events list.

> 10.17 a.m – Call from LoCost (major supermarket) reporting complaints from three stores of contamination of food products. Contamination looks like bits of building materials/plaster and all are from Monday's date code (use by 17 July). They want all this day's code date product withdrawn and want to conduct a site visit tomorrow to discuss the issue and inspect the stock.

This started the contamination story, added information and introduced pressure with an impending site visit.

> 10.19 a.m – Further information reveals that on Sunday, a hygiene crew came in to the plant to clean and prepare for production but found that the contractors were still working and there were many exposed wall surfaces and panels. In addition there was still debris around the working areas. Elsewhere, as a quick fix solution, holes and gaps were sealed with waterproof tape and cleaning commenced. During cleaning, the tape came away exposing holes and the inner contents of the wall panels and dislodged more debris. However, as the contractors had left the site by then, production commenced.

This added more information for the team to act on.

> 10:21 – CEO has heard about the complaints from LoCost. He's busy but wants briefing on the situation by phone at 11.00 a.m (in 40 mins).

This introduced the requirement to brief, added some time pressure and gave the team a definite goal to aim for.

> 10.25 a.m – 20 names of what are said to be illegal immigrants are identified at the plant. Can the site prepare for a visit from Home Office tomorrow afternoon to interview staff with a view to checking their legal status?

This added to the problems and gave human resources a headache.

> 10.27 a.m – Call from local reporter saying she has just heard about contaminated food at LoCost – anything to do with Brighter Meats?

This introduced local media interest and tested whether the policy of referring all press enquiries to the external PR firm was followed.

The session ended with a briefing to the CEO, which concentrated the team's thoughts on reviewing and summarizing what had happened, the actions they had taken and what direction they required.

To ensure that any lessons identified were carried forward into the following session, a hot wash-up was held in the final 10 minutes of each session.

The discussion identified that some roles and responsibilities within the team were not fully understood and the requirement to run an 'incident log' was not fully appreciated.

The second session

The second session assumed a time jump to the following day and involved more reports of product contamination and the failure of a newly installed piece of equipment resulting in the partial loss of production for seven days. It started with a simulated video news broadcast, which introduced new aspects to the scenario and captured the players' attention from the outset.

> Good morning, you're watching News One.
>
> LoCost has today cleared some of its shelves following the discovery that a batch of their meat products are contaminated.
>
> The alarm was raised yesterday when customers discovered pork chops and chicken breasts coated in a fine white powder.
>
> News One has spoken to one shopper who bought meat products from a store in Birmingham and in her words 'it was covered in what looked like plaster or brick dust.'
>
> We invited LoCost on to the programme, but no one was available.
>
> However, they told us that all contaminated products appear to bear the same date code and that all products with this code have been removed from their shelves.
>
> They say they're trying to establish the cause of the problem but in the mean time are urging shoppers to be vigilant and are offering a full and immediate refund on all products found to be contaminated.

> If you've had a problem with LoCost food products then we want to hear about it – so please get in touch.
>
> You're watching News One.

This brought the problem into the public domain although Brighter Meats was not, as yet, directly linked with the contamination. More injections built on the contamination scenario and introduced the failure of a vital item of newly installed equipment.

> 11:17 – Call from LoCost saying they have received complaints from customers at more stores concerning similar contamination of meat products. They are sending samples to the Campden Food Research Association for analysis. They are instigating a public recall of all meat products with the Monday date code.

This indicated that the contamination had not been contained and increased pressure because of the public recall. It also challenged the players to prepare for what the food analysis might bring to light.

> 11.21 a.m – Member of staff calls saying he had noticed during the last couple of days that newly installed equipment was a bit temperamental and it now seems to have seized completely. Someone said it was damaged when it was put in. A quick inspection has revealed several broken components and the initial estimate is seven days to repair.

This introduced the equipment malfunction and gave an estimated down time thereby setting the timescales for the team.

> 11.25 a.m – CEO has heard about the equipment failure. He wants the gold team to convene at 11.55 a.m. At that time he requests a full brief on the situation by audio conference call. In particular production, supply, delivery to customers, work force, etc.

Delivering the exercise

This introduced the need for a briefing and gave the team the issues to concentrate on. Shortly afterwards a second news broadcast was played, which put the company's name firmly in the public domain.

Good morning, this is News One.

And it looks like a local firm could be responsible for the food contamination at LoCost.

Brighter Meats has a processing plant which is currently undergoing refurbishment and the suspicion is the contamination may have come from building dust at their premises.

Employees talk of construction work releasing a considerable amount of dust and debris.

The factory continues to operate, but one of its two production lines has been shut – not for safety reasons, but because of equipment failure.

The factory processes a huge amount of meat products and with one production line closed, lorries full of animals are starting to build up outside the plant – animal rights groups are already voicing their concern.

Brighter Meats is sending workers home and some are complaining that as they're from Eastern Europe they're the first to go and have few rights.

One member of staff from Estonia, who wouldn't reveal his name, claimed that in its drive to cut costs the company regularly employ illegal workers from outside the EU.

The majority of Brighter Meat's products go to LoCost who are known to demand exacting standards from their suppliers. Analysts say the company needs to get its act together quickly or face the wrath of one of the world's biggest retailers.

While the silver team continued with the exercise, the gold team were given an introductory brief by silver on an audio conference call before they joined the exercise.

After this briefing the CEO wanted the involvement of their PR company to deal with media issues. This was unexpected as the exercise was to have been kept in

---

house. However, the PR company was called and after a quick introductory brief, joined in the exercise play. This demonstrated the value of being dynamic and the need for flexibility.

A working lunch was provided between sessions 2 and 3.

The third session

The final session assumed another time jump to the following day and centred on the fact that the contamination was of such severity that the entire plant could be closed from one to three months. During the session the silver team were tasked with considering the issues of a one month closure while the gold team looked at the longer term aspects of a three month shut down. It started with a situation update briefing by the facilitators, which specifically included instructions for what was required of each team. While slightly artificial, this focussed the minds of the players and was necessary to achieve the exercise objectives.

12.15 p.m – The exercise date is now Thursday. Scenario update. Results from the Campden food analysis reveal that the food samples contained quantities of wall plaster, brick dust but more importantly, asbestos fibres. In view of this, Brighter Meats informed the Food Standards Agency which ordered a full investigation and rescinded the license to operate until the asbestos had been completely removed.

Following initial investigations at Brighter Meats it is believed that the asbestos came from the new wall panels that had been supplied to the wrong specification. It is anticipated that it will take about one month to remove and replace all the wall panels and carry out a full decontamination of the entire site.

Specific requirements – silver to consider the implications of a one month closure and provide a brief for gold at 1.05 p.m with an outline plan in particular production, supply, customers, workforce, refurbishment project. Gold to consider options if closure is extended to three months.

After 10 minutes, a third news broadcast was played which reported the progressively worsening contamination problem from a local to a national perspective. This escalated the reputation issues and fully engaged the PR company.

> Good morning, this is News One.
>
> Brighter Meats the company at the centre of the LoCost food scare face a new crisis today.
>
> The Health and Safety Executive in conjunction with the Food Standards Agency have closed one of their factories following the discovery of traces of asbestos.
>
> Building work is believed to have released asbestos into the air and it's understood the factory will be shut for at least a month while decontamination takes place.
>
> But experts warn this type of work is notoriously difficult and could take as long as six months.
>
> Employees have spoken of building work releasing clouds of dust into the plant. Many are concerned that the dust contained asbestos – well known for causing cancer.
>
> Over 900 workers have been sent home without pay, which will severely impact the local economy. Many are from Eastern Europe and will have difficulty claiming unemployment benefit.
>
> Union officials are demanding workers be paid while laid off and want full health monitoring for those who may have been exposed to asbestos. Closure of this plant will likely have repercussions well beyond the factory gates.

The session again ended with a briefing on the situation to the gold team.

Due to the thorough planning and preparation the exercise went completely according to plan with the exception of the late inclusion of the PR company. The pace allowed the players to consider the issues in detail without being rushed and to interact with the scenario cell who responded realistically and dynamically.

Hot wash-up

After the final session, 45 minutes were allocated to allow a full discussion of all the lessons and shortcomings identified. All recognized the value of conducting such exercises and were grateful for the short debriefs after sessions one and two allowing lessons identified to be carried forward.

Player feedback

The players were also invited to complete a feedback form that sought their views on various aspects of the BCP, their perceived performance of the team and their overall impressions of the exercise.

Table 4.1

Item	Issue	Requirement	Recommended Action
1	Team members are not familiar with the plan.	Team members need to be briefed on the plan, made aware of their roles and responsibilities and be given some simple tools to support them in their role.	An annual workshop run jointly for the gold and silver incident management teams.
2	For exercise purposes the silver team were gathered in one place at an agreed time. How this would happen in reality needs to be considered.	There is a need to establish if the activation process would work, and how and where a first 'meeting' of the Silver Team would take place.	An activation exercise that establishes if all team members can be contacted, confirms what the default meeting process is for the initial 'meeting' and establishes an opening agenda.
3	The recording of critical information, decisions and actions needs to be formalized.	Establish procedures for recording of key information, decisions and actions. Establish the facility to display the recorded data. Establish the capability to update the data and integrate this with the team review process.	1. Confirm the requirement including the need to display information as part of the review process. 2. Document procedures and processes. 3. Train support personnel. 4. Develop capability through exercises.

Written report

A detailed report on the exercise was written from the facilitators' observations, their benchmarking comments and the players' observations. The report highlighted areas of the plan and procedures that required amendment or implementation and concluded with an action plan suggesting how the improvements could be made.

Key points

What are the key points that can be drawn from this case study?

- Build a realistic and challenging scenario
- The quality of an injection in the master events list is far more important than the quantity
- Teams can be in different locations
- Teams or individual players need not participate in the whole exercise
- Exercises can be used to test a company's response to real live issues as well as those raised by a hypothetical scenario
- Time jumps can be easily achieved during exercises
- The scenario cell needs to be dynamic and flexible.

5. Reporting and evaluation

'We are drowning in information but starved for knowledge'. John Naisbitt (writer and business philosopher)

Writing the exercise report

The exercise is over, and as you followed this book's advice you can look with pride at the player feedback forms, which clearly show that those involved thought it a resounding success. However, the job is not quite complete.

As an organization you will have invested considerable resources in your exercise. Now is the time to confirm the value of the event to your senior leadership and all those who took part. A comprehensive report is called for, which must reflect what took place on the day and be linked clearly to the exercise aims and objectives. Only by doing this will your organization be able to plot a way forward. Once completed, the report should provide you with the evidence that will:

- Identify amendments to your existing incident management plan, supporting procedures and processes
- Alternatively, identify requirements for producing a new plan
- Identify and justify future training requirements for individuals and teams
- Identify and justify additional resources to enhance your current capability
- Identify objectives for future exercises
- Provide audit evidence of the effectiveness of your approach to incident management.

This section will outline the component parts of a flexible framework for reporting different types of exercises and workshops.

Dependent on your requirements you should consider what parts are required and adjust the contents to your situation and circumstances.

Key issues

Report format and presentation

As part of the exercise planning process you should discuss with senior management or the project sponsor what the format of the report will look like and once information has been gathered how it should be presented. Planning and agreeing your report format should be seen as an integrated part of the planning process and should be considered from the outset and then reviewed as the exercise planning develops.

Types of report

A simple exercise may only require a summary of conclusions and findings together with an agreed action plan.

For example, you may wish to test the activation of your incident management plan. Looking at the statements in Table 5.1 you will be able to report with a simple yes or no, backed by observed evidence, whether the plans and procedures worked. An example is shown in Table 5.1.

Table 5.1

ACTIVATION		
The plan	**Yes**	**No**
The BCP details procedures and process for activation of the incident management structure		
Contact details are documented and correct		
Team members could be contacted and understood their role and responsibility		
The first team meeting took place within the required time frame		

Medium and complex exercises will require a more detailed report and will feature most of the elements contained within this chapter.

The key is to agree the format and style with senior executives prior to the event taking place.

Collecting feedback from the participants

Participants will have a view on how they and their team performed and the strengths and weaknesses of the plan, if one exists. This is valuable information. It should be captured as soon as possible, ideally at the end of the exercise.

For a simple exercise it may be enough to conduct a debrief to capture participants thoughts while they are still fresh. Participants or team leaders, if many people are involved, can typically be asked to make three points – what is good about the organization's processes and procedures, what is bad and what must be changed.

For a medium or complex exercise it will be necessary to prepare a form which will enable facilitators to gather feedback from the players before they return to their normal jobs and the exercise becomes a distant memory.

Feedback format

A feedback form or questionnaire has the advantage of obtaining detailed feedback from all the players rather than just those who volunteer their views. Additionally once completed, the results can be entered into a spreadsheet and presented in your report – highlighting particular themes in a very effective manner. (An example of this can be found in the case study at the end of the chapter.)

The feedback form shown in Table 5.2 provides an illustration of one approach and, as with the exercise criteria, should be adapted to your individual requirements.

The report

Executive summary

Your senior leadership team will want to know:

- Did the exercise achieve the aims and objectives? A short statement is required that summarizes the exercise, the overall performance of the teams and the effectiveness of the plan
- What were the key findings? Select the two or three key themes that emerged during post exercise analysis

- What are the main recommendations? The recommendations will be those you would like the executive to support so that future enhancements to your current capability can take place.

Table 5.2

ITEM	COMMUNICATION	Strongly disagree	Disagree	Don't know	Agree	Strongly agree
1.1	The teams have established communications protocols, and robust and reliable systems with which to communicate.					
1.2	Key external audiences, messages and preferred communication channels have been identified.					
1.3	Effective internal communications channels and protocols for disseminating information to 'our people' have been established.					
1.4	The procedures and processes for communicating with the media are effective.					
1.5	Comment (additional comments on Communications).					
ITEM 2	INFORMATION MANAGEMENT	Strongly disagree	Disagree	Don't know	Agree	Strongly agree
2.1	The team relays information accurately.					
2.2	The team builds and maintains an informed picture of the situation.					
2.3	The flow of information into the IMT is sufficiently swift to support timely decision-making.					

		Strongly disagree	Disagree	Don't know	Agree	Strongly agree
2.4	The team has a process to record incoming and outgoing information.					
2.5	The team shares information effectively.					
2.6	The team members effectively share information.					
2.7	The team conducts regular reviews to maintain a current picture of the situation.					
2.8	The team has an information recording process that would have supported an effective audit trail.					
2.9	Comment (additional comments on information management).					
ITEM 3	**DECISION MAKING**	Strongly disagree	Disagree	Don't know	Agree	Strongly agree
3.1	The team understood their role and responsibilities.					
3.2	The team approach to decision making was effective.					
3.3	The team decisions were translated into actions and tasks.					
3.4	The team has a process for monitoring ongoing actions and tasks.					
3.5	The team has a process for recording decisions, actions and tasks.					
3.6	The team decision-making procedures and processes would have supported an effective audit trail.					
3.7	Comment (additional comments on decision making).					

ITEM 4	THE EXERCISE	Strongly disagree	Disagree	Don't know	Agree	Strongly agree
4.1	The exercise achieved the exercise objectives.					
4.2	The exercise helped develop my personal confidence as a team member.					
4.3	The exercise identified that I need more training in my role and responsibilities.					
4.4	The exercise was well-organized.					
4.5	Comment (additional comments on the exercise organization and delivery).					

Main body

The main body of the report should cover your observations in some detail. How best to obtain this information needs some thought. The exercise director, the scenario cell manager and particularly the facilitators can gather a large proportion of it.

One approach is to focus attention on the four component parts of an effective response to incident management: activation, communications, information management and decision making (sometimes known as the ACID test of an organization's capability). Each of the components can be broken down into the key criteria they involve and be effectively benchmarked using the traffic light approach – red, amber and green.

Using traffic lights

The colour of the traffic light indicates the overall status of each particular exercise criteria. Each colour is supported by a definition and meaning that will provide those who read the report with an understanding and an indication of areas that require attention. The suggested traffic light definitions are shown in Table 5.3.

Table 5.3

Colour	Definition	Meaning
Green	The individual or team performed consistently at the level of efficiency required for the successful delivery of a capable response to a major incident.	Regular practise should be programmed to maintain performance levels.
Amber	The individual or team achieved most tasks to a satisfactory standard, though the overall level of performance was degraded by errors in the use of established procedures, or from the lack of effective procedures.	Further training or the development of procedures, followed by assessment, should be scheduled as part of the ongoing programme.
Red	The individual or team performance consistently fell below the standard required to respond effectively to a major incident, either through a lack of use of established procedures, or through the absence of such procedures.	Urgent remedial action is required.

Briefing facilitators

Facilitators are central to the smooth running of an exercise. They are also uniquely placed to gather information from the participants – during the exercise they become your eyes and ears. In order that they understand what you require of them they will need careful briefing and detailed direction. Providing them, prior to the event, with an ACID test form, will help them deliver evidence-based observations.

Table 5.4 shows a sample of questions designed to benchmark an organization's communication skills. The case study in this chapter contains a full assessment form, which includes questions on all other elements of the ACID test.

Referring to the aims and objectives of your exercise you should use those you wish to report on and add your own criteria as appropriate. The evidence column contains detailed observations by you and your facilitators and should be as objective as possible. Supporting evidence is of particular importance when amber or red is shown.

Table 5.4 – Combining the traffic lights with the communication criteria

	Green	Amber	Red	Evidence
2.0 COMMUNICATIONS PLAN				
2.1 Communications Plan				
2.1.1 A communications plan has been prepared and is understood.				
2.1.2 The communication strategy identifies the importance of protecting the organization's reputation.				
2.1.3 The plan includes pre-prepared communication templates.				
2.2 External Relationships				
2.2.1 The plan documents the requirements of the Regulators and the team delivers them.				
2.2.2 The plan documents the requirements of the local authorities and the team delivers them.				
2.2.3 The plan documents the requirements of the emergency services and the team delivers them.				
2.2.4 The plan documents key stakeholder requirements and the team delivers them.				

	Green	Amber	Red	Evidence
2.3 Internal				
2.3.1 The procedures and processes for communicating with staff and their relatives are in place and understood.				
2.3.2 The procedures and processes for communicating internally can respond to a fast-moving situation.				
2.3.3 Staff received regular and accurate communications.				
2.4 Media				
2.4.1 The procedures and processes for responding to media enquiries are effective.				
2.4.2 The procedures for monitoring multiple media sources are effective.				
2.4.3 The procedures and processes for responding to media requests for interviews are effective.				
2.4.4 The procedures for preparing senior executives to talk to the media are effective.				
2.4.5 The procedures for preparing and running a media conference are effective.				

Main recommendations or action plan

Purpose

In Section 1 we outlined the importance of using the workshop or exercise to plan the way forward. The action plan does this by summarizing the issues, establishing the requirement, making recommendations for actions and detailing ownership. It effectively completes one event and begins the process for the next.

Action plan format

An outline format and an example of how an issue could be approached is shown in Table 5.5.

Table 5.5

Item	Issue	Requirement	Recommended actions	Owner	Target date
1	Record Keeping	1. Establish procedures for recording of key information, decisions and actions 2. Establish the facility to display the recorded data 3. Establish the capability to update the data and integrate this with the team review process	1. Confirm the requirement including need to display information for review processes 2. Develop procedures and processes 3. Train support personnel 4. Develop capability through exercises	BC Manager	End of March

Presentation

Writing a report can sometimes seem a daunting task, but reading a badly prepared report can be equally demoralizing. Unless a report is presented in a clear and interesting fashion no one will want to read it.

Use headings or headlines as signposts to guide the reader. These will help them assimilate the findings quickly by highlighting the main points. Use phrases like, 'the aim of this report is to…' or 'this section deals with…' If you are reaching a conclusion then make it clear, 'the result shows that…' or perhaps, 'this means that…'.

The reader will not be interested in a long narrative of what happened on the day – just enough to set the scene for those that weren't present. What they will want are the key findings and the action plan.

If you are emailing the report to a senior executive put the key findings in the body of the email so the executive does not have to open the attachment to read them. If they are sufficiently interesting – and if you have done your job properly they will be – this will act as an incentive for the recipient to read the whole report rather than putting it to one side. Finally, a report should not be seen as a completion but rather as a step on a continuous quest for greater resilience. Gather support for the report's findings, implement the changes and move your organization forward.

Case study

This chapter explored the elements that make up a successful exercise report. The case study looks at a completed report to enable you to see how all the component parts fit together.

First of all, here is a little background to the exercise on which the report is based. For the purpose of this book the company undertaking the exercise is called ABC Financial Services.

Client brief

To conduct a real-time, scenario based, major incident management exercise. The focus: the ABC Financial Services Incident Management Team (IMT).

Exercise purpose

To assess the preparedness of ABC Financial Services IMT to manage the effects of a major incident, both on colleagues and on the business.

Specific objectives

- To establish the current level of incident management performance
- To introduce new members of the IMT to their role and responsibilities.

Format

The exercise was a real-time medium scale simulation exercise involving a coordinated protest action against ABC Financial Services. Both the company's employees and property will be targeted. The main location of the actions will be at the company's headquarters office. The exercise will use a scenario cell, video news clips and simulated news websites to build a virtual environment within which the exercise can take place.

Scenario

A coordinated attack on ABC Financial Services designed to cause significant reputational and operational impact in order to promote their activist group's agenda.

INCIDENT MANAGEMENT EXERCISE
For ABC Financial Services Incident Management Team
CONFIDENTIAL REPORT

Table of Contents

Section 1 – Executive Summary

Overall assessment

Our findings confirm the appropriateness of the approach of the incident management team (IMT) to developing and maintaining an incident management capability. Refinements to existing procedures and processes and the maintenance of the team's collective skills will reinforce the team's preparedness to respond effectively to a major incident.

Key findings

During a major incident a fully resourced communications team will be essential to delivering an effective response.

The communications team understands its role but is under resourced. The communications representative needs to be supported by a team that can coordinate the delivery of both external and internal communications.

The IMT needs better information management tools.

The IMT benefited from strong leadership during the exercise, which generated a dynamic and coordinated response. Given that the team leader may change, processes and procedures need to be documented. In particular we recommend that a meeting agenda, a format for conducting situation reviews, and information and decision making recording methods need to be agreed and documented.

Recommendations

- Establish a communications team to support the IMT communications representative
- Fully document the opening agenda, a situation review process and the process for recording critical information and decision making

Section 2 – The Report

Introduction

Aim

The aim of this report is to outline the observations made during the recent incident management exercise and to identify an action plan that will reinforce ABC Financial Services Incident Management capability.

The exercise

The brief was to conduct a real-time scenario based simulation exercise focused on the incident management team. The purpose was to establish the readiness level of the team to manage the effects of a major incident.

Report format

Section 1

An executive summary with key findings and recommendations.

Section 2

Performance report

An analysis based on the agreed exercise criteria. The status is indicated by the 'green, amber, red' traffic light format.

Player feedback

The collated data gathered from the feedback forms completed by all players at the end of the exercise.

Action Plan

The key issues identified as requiring further action.

Performance Report

Table 5.R1

	Green	Amber	Red	Evidence
Communications				
1.1 Internal				
1.1.1 The procedures and processes for communicating with staff and their relatives are in place and understood.				Not tested.

1.1.2 The procedures and processes for communicating internally can respond to a fast moving situation.				The use of pre-prepared templates will enhance the capability of the team to respond to fast-moving situations.
1.1.3 Staff received regular and accurate communications.				This was discussed. The process for this to take place is understood.
1.2 Media				
1.2.1 The procedures and processes for responding to media enquiries are effective.				The team understood the need to defer all media requests for information. Additional personnel are required to support the communications representative. This is in order to deal with the anticipated volume of media enquiries and need to communicate with customers. A communications team should be established which reports back into the IMT through the communications representative.
Information Management				
2.1 The plan				
2.1.1 The team are aware of the business approach to incident management.				Yes.

2.1.2 The team understand the incident management structure.				It was noted that at the start of the meeting it would be useful to confirm individual responsibilities for the benefit of new members.
2.2 Accuracy				
2.2.1 The team analyse information in order to build and then maintain an accurate picture of the emerging situation.				Yes but the review process needs to ensure that all information is reviewed.
2.2.2 The team identify and correct misinformation.				Yes. This was done well.
3.3 Timeliness				
3.3.1 The team recognize the importance of time when handling and forwarding time critical information.				Yes.
3.3.2 The team establish a disciplined rhythm for collecting and analyzing information.				This steadily improved as the exercise developed.
3.4 Effective recording				
3.4.1 The team have a process to record incoming and outgoing information.				Yes, but the process and means need to be formalized to ensure all key information is captured and accurately recorded.

3.5 Effective use

| 3.5.1 The team members effectively share information between themselves. | | | | Yes. |

3.6 Effective review

| 3.6.1 The team conduct regular reviews to determine a current picture of the situation. | | | | Reviews took place regularly under the direction of the team leader. |

3.7 Audit

| 3.7.1 The information recording procedures and processes would have provided an effective audit trail. | | | | This was not well done. Though information was recorded, it was difficult to follow how, when and why decisions were made. |

DECISION MAKING

4.1 Roles and responsibilities

| 4.1.1 The team understand their role and responsibilities for decision making. | | | | The team leader became the focus for all key decision making. This worked for a short exercise but a number of team members were concerned that over a protracted period the team leader could be overwhelmed. Team members noted that increased use of collective decision-making would enhance overall situation awareness among the team and reduce the pressure on the team leader. |

4.1.2 The individual team members understand their role.				Yes.
4.1.3 The team understood the limitations or constraints placed upon them.				The exercise reinforced the need to recognize the primacy of the emergency services and to accept their advice.
4.1.4 The team understand and remain compliant with legal and regulatory requirements .				Yes.
4.2 Timeliness				
4.2.1 When appropriate the team leader identifies the need for timely decision making.				Yes. This was done well.
4.2.2 The team's approach to decision-making supports timely decision-making in time critical situations.				Individual team members recognized the need for timely decision making, which they subsequently confirmed with the team leader.
4.3 Dissemination of decisions				
4.3.1 The decisions taken get translated into actions and tasks.				The scenario cell noted that the IMT were not clear what actions and tasks were required of them as representatives of their business areas.

4.3.2 These actions and tasks get communicated swiftly to the appropriate supporting "action" teams.

The scenario cell noted that they were not back briefed on the emerging situation and would have found it difficult to identify which priorities had precedence.

Player Feedback

Action Plan

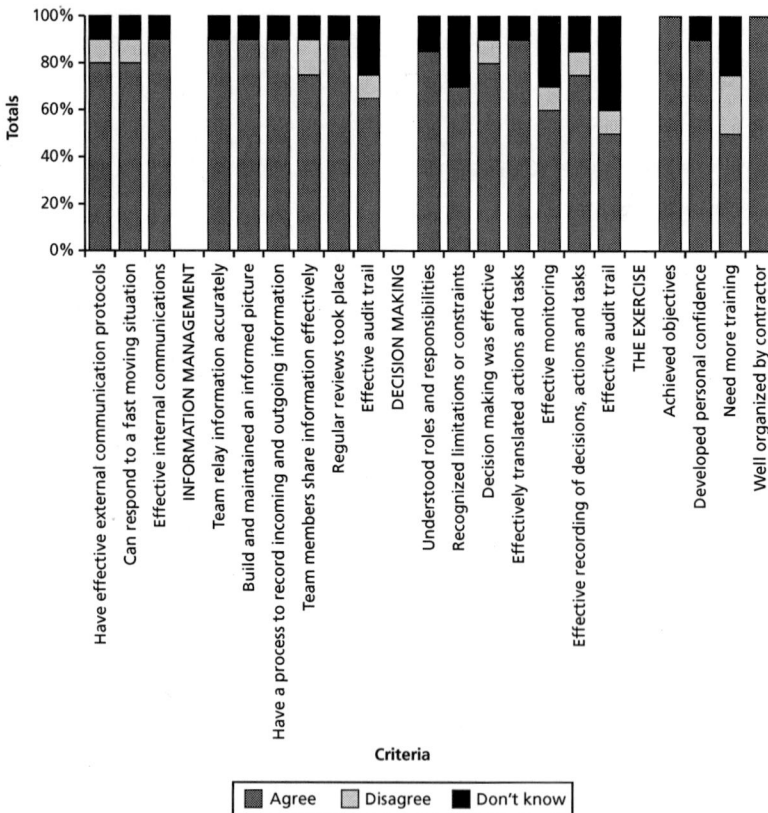

Legend: Agree — Disagree — Don't know

X-axis (Criteria):

- Have effective external communication protocols
- Can respond to a fast moving situation
- Effective internal communications
- INFORMATION MANAGEMENT
- Team relay information accurately
- Build and maintained an informed picture
- Have a process to record incoming and outgoing information
- Team members share information effectively
- Regular reviews took place
- Effective audit trail
- DECISION MAKING
- Understood roles and responsibilities
- Recognized limitations or constraints
- Decision making was effective
- Effectively translated actions and tasks
- Effective monitoring
- Effective recording of decisions, actions and tasks
- Effective audit trail
- THE EXERCISE
- Achieved objectives
- Developed personal confidence
- Need more training
- Well organized by contractor

Y-axis (Totals): 0%, 20%, 40%, 60%, 80%, 100%

Issue	Requirement	Recommended Actions	Owner	Target Date
Incident management procedures	The team's approach to Incident Management needs to be documented. Develop and agree an opening agenda and situation review format.	Agree content and format. Document within the current plan. Practise in future exercises.		
Communications planning	Establish a communications team responsible for coordinating all internal and external messages and media enquires.	Identify appropriate personnel. Run a communications workshop.		
Record keeping	Establish procedures for recording of key information, decisions and actions. Establish the facility to display the recorded data. Establish the capability to update the data and integrate this with the team review process.	Confirm the requirement including the format required, and how it can best be presented. Document the procedures and processes. Train support personnel.		

What have I learnt from this chapter?

- Senior management should be involved in determining the report format
- You must brief your facilitators on what you require and where to focus their attention
- The report should be as objective as possible
- Shortcomings in your plan or in the performance of individuals should be supported by evidence
- The report should signpost the way forward through the inclusion of an action plan.

Glossary of terms and abbreviations

BCM – business continuity management or business continuity manager.

BCP – business continuity plan.

Call cascade – a pre-defined means of contacting all members of the crisis management teams both in and out of working hours.

CMT – crisis management team (some organizations refer to it as an incident management team).

DR site – disaster recovery site – an off-site facility to which nominated staff go in the event of being denied access to their offices. The nominated staff are usually those required to continue business critical activities. Will normally contain or have access to back-up computer systems.

EPG – exercise planning group.

EPMT – exercise programme management team.

ETD – exercise telephone directory – will contain all the telephone numbers (including fax and email addresses) that are used during the exercise.

Exercise director – individual in charge of the exercise on the day of delivery.

Exercise time – the time at which the exercise is deemed to be running. For example actual time may be 9.00 a.m, but in the virtual world of the exercise the time is 1.00 p.m.

Facilitator – an individual who oversees and aids a particular team during exercise play. Facilitators should help ensure the smooth running of an exercise. They will liaise with the scenario cell manager and the exercise director.

Gold, silver and bronze crisis/incident management teams – gold would normally be very senior management. Silver would often be executives on the crisis management team (CMT). Bronze would be those implementing actions on the ground. Sometimes useful to think in terms of the roles of gold, silver and bronze as, Think (strategic) – Plan (tactical) – Do (operational).

Glossary of terms and abbreviations

Hot wash-up/debrief – a plenary session of all participants immediately following the exercise to capture lessons and issues identified during the exercise and provide an initial assessment of performance.

IMT – incident management team (some organizations refer to it as the crisis management team).

Injection – individual piece of dynamic information contained in the master events list.

Lead planner – individual in charge of planning the exercise.

MEL – master/main events list – a series of dynamic injections that drive a simulated scenario.

Participant's instructions – a document sent to all participants in advance of the exercise telling them where and when they are required and any preparations they should make prior to the exercise.

Participant's feedback forms – the players' chance to vent their feelings about all aspects of the exercise in a pre-agreed, pre-prepared questionnaire.

RAG report – red, amber, green system of benchmarking. Also known as the traffic light approach.

Scenario cell – a group of people who represent the outside world to the exercise participants and deliver the dynamic injections that drive the scenario.

SCM – scenario cell manager.

Start state – information given to the players regarding the scenario at the beginning of the exercise. Often delivered verbally by the CMT chairperson from a prepared script using a PowerPoint presentation.

Traffic light approach also known as a RAG Report – the Red, Amber, Green system of benchmarking.

Virtual world – the environment, both physical and intellectual in which the exercise takes place.